Potty Training for Boys in 3 Days

A Step-by-Step Guide with Tips and Tricks for Modern Busy Parents to Potty Train Their Toddlers

Stephany Hicks

© **Copyright 2020 - All rights reserved.**

The content contained within this book may not be reproduced, duplicated or transmitted without direct written permission from the author or the publisher.

Under no circumstances will any blame or legal responsibility be held against the publisher, or author, for any damages, reparation, or monetary loss due to the information contained within this book, either directly or indirectly.

Legal Notice:

This book is copyright protected. It is only for personal use. You cannot amend, distribute, sell, use, quote or paraphrase any part, or the content within this book, without the consent of the author or publisher.

Disclaimer Notice:

Please note the information contained within this document is for educational and entertainment purposes only. All effort has been executed to present accurate, up to date, reliable, complete information. No warranties of any kind are declared or implied. Readers acknowledge that the author is not engaged in the rendering of legal, financial, medical or professional advice. The content within this book has been derived from various sources. Please consult a licensed professional before attempting any techniques outlined in this book.

By reading this document, the reader agrees that under no circumstances is the author responsible for any losses, direct or indirect, that are incurred as a result of the use of the information contained within this document, including, but not limited to, errors, omissions, or inaccuracies.

Table of Contents

INTRODUCTION	1
THE PROBLEM	5
THE SOLUTION	6
About Stephany Hicks	7
CHAPTER 1: TAKING THE FIRST STEP	**9**
HOW DO I KNOW MY SON IS READY FOR TOILET TRAINING?	10
Indicators to Look Out For	12
WHY CHOOSE THE 3-DAY METHOD?	18
It Doesn't Interfere Much With Schedules	19
It Minimizes Frustration	19
It Avoids Subjecting Your Child To Conflicting Training	20
WHAT IS NEEDED TO USE THE 3-DAY METHOD?	20
3 Full Days of the Parents' Time	21
The Right Mindset	22
A Potty Chair or Add-on Seat	23
New Underpants	24
Rewards	24
The Right Diet	25
Three, two, one...	25
HOW WILL THIS BOOK HELP YOU?	25
CHAPTER 2: POTTY TRAINING MYTHS AND MISCONCEPTIONS	**27**
COMMON MYTHS	28
You Should Ask Your Son Often If He Needs to Go	29
You Should Set a Timer to Have Your Child Go to the Bathroom Regularly	31
If Your Child Tells You He Has Gone in His Diaper, He is Ready to Potty Train Right Away	32
Rewards are Necessary for Effective Toilet Training	33
Girls are Easier to Train Than Boys	34
Your Son Will Tell You When He's Ready	35
Daycare Will Potty Train Your Child	37
You Should Not Let Your Child Wear Diapers Once They Start Toilet Training	38
COMMON TRUTHS	39
CHAPTER 3: PREPARATION	**45**
PREPARING YOUR SON	46
Start Educating Him	47

Get Him Excited About It	49
PARENTAL PREPARATION	50
Schedule the Weekend	50
Go On a Potty-Themed Shopping Spree	52
Come Up With a "Well Done" Action	53
Stock Up on Supplies	54

CHAPTER 4: DAY ONE — 59

STEP 1 - START YOUR DAY FIRST	62
STEP 2 - GET HIM EXCITED ABOUT IT	63
STEP 3 - EXPLAIN THE BASICS	64
STEP 4 - BE ATTENTIVE	65
THINGS TO REMEMBER	66
Accidents WILL Happen	66
Praise Him When He Does It Right	67
Be Thoughtful of How You Phrase Things	68
Make Sure Your Son is Ready Before Beginning	68

CHAPTER 5: DAYS TWO AND THREE — 71

STEPS TO FOLLOW THROUGH THE DAY	73
Keep Him Hydrated & Eating	74
Keep an Eye on Him	75
Get Him to the Bathroom Quickly (When He Needs to Go)	76
Make Sure There Are No Distractions	77
THINGS TO KEEP IN MIND	78
Hand Washing	79
Wiping	80
Imitation	81
Positive Reinforcement	82
GETTING OUT OF THE HOUSE	84
Prepare	85
Be Quick	87
Be Calm	88

CHAPTER 6: GOING FORWARD — 91

OBSERVE	92
LET IT EVOLVE	93
EXPECT ACCIDENTS	94
What to Do	96
REGRESSION	97
What to Do	98

COMMON PROBLEMS (AND SOLUTIONS)	100
Your Son Doesn't Recognize When He Needs to Pee	*101*
He Resists Going to the Bathroom	*102*
He's Afraid of the Toilet	*102*
He Tries to Play With His Pee or Poop	*103*
He'll Only Go to the Toilet With One Particular Person	*104*
CONCLUSION	**107**
REFERENCES	**109**

Introduction

When I first became a parent I was overjoyed. My husband and I had spent many months preparing our home for our new baby. We painted the nursery, bought a beautiful crib, and stocked up on diapers. We went to birthing classes, shopped for maternity clothing, and ate for two...together (he's super supportive!).

When the time came, we sped off to the hospital with a mixture of anxiety and excitement. 4 hours later, our son was born. He was the most beautiful little human I'd ever laid eyes on. He had his daddy's nose, right off the bat. I hoped he'd have his green eyes, too.

The months that followed were a bit of a blur. I recall the extreme joy of having my own little family, the three of us spending time together bonding. I can remember sitting next to my sleeping baby boy for hours, just watching his tiny face and marveling at the fact that this gorgeous little person was literally a piece of me and my husband.

I also remember not having much sleep, but we were so over the moon with our beautiful son that we didn't even mind waking up to look after him. He was a lovely baby from the very beginning, though, and slept through the night very quickly. I know! We were extremely lucky - many parents struggle heavily with this aspect of having a new baby.

But there was one thing—just one—that haunted my days, nights, and dreams. If I got even a hint of it, hubby had to come to the rescue. If I even caught sight of it, I swooned.

It was the poop.

I mean, I knew babies pooped a lot. That's pretty well-covered in parenting classes. But I was completely unprepared for the reality of changing diapers and being *that* close and personal.

Over the years, I did get used to it. It's kind of hard not to when you're changing diapers every day, multiple times a day! But let me tell you, I was ever so glad when it came time to potty-train my little boy.

Some parents dread this particular milestone. For some, it's the first real transition away from being your baby and into being a real little human of their own. It can be rough!

To be honest, I thought potty training would be a breeze. Put him on the toilet, give him a reward when he was done, and next time he'd know exactly how to do it. As for number one, well, that was dad's duty. I don't know how to aim from that angle.

As I'm sure you can imagine, it didn't go quite as planned. It took *months* to get it right. I started feeling like I was letting my baby down. This is something mom's supposed to teach, right? What if I fail, and he has to wear diapers forever? Irrational fears, yes, but that's how it felt when I was washing yet another pair of soiled underwear and wondering if I needed more diapers.

You'll be glad to know that my son eventually did learn how to do the thing, and is now a happy, healthy, fully toilet-trained college boy. But at the time it sure felt like a nightmare. And just as it seemed to be a complete thing of the past, son number two reached that stage.

The memories of the first time around came flooding back. I was determined not to make the same mistakes (but also slightly less nervous that he would be untrained for life). Guess what? It took about half the time to potty-train him as it did my first.

By the time child number three, my daughter, came along, I figured I had this down to a fine art. Training a girl is a little different, but it was more my thing anyway, being a mommy and not a daddy. She learned quickly, thankfully - in fact, in just a weekend. I wrote about this experience in my girl-centered book, "Potty Training for Girls in 3 Days." If you have a daughter around potty-training age, you may find some useful info in there!

By now I had three successfully potty-trained children under my belt. Sure, I had done it differently with each one. And of course there had been moments of regression, accidents had happened, and there had been plenty of tears (from children and mom).

But I had done it! The milestone that seemed so huge in the beginning was passed and although I had tried multiple different techniques, tips, and tricks, eventually each of my kids had learned, and in far less time than I anticipated. I, too, had learned things along the way. I was prepared to put poop and potties behind me.

I had sailed through a few accident-free months quite happily. It was a sunny Saturday, and my best friend and her family were visiting for a barbecue. We were sipping wine, the men were grilling, and the kids were playing, when her little boy came running. He'd had a bit of an accident, and mom apologized profusely and took him off to be cleaned up.

When she came back, she shared with me how she'd been struggling to potty-train her son. Well, memories came flooding back. Over glass of wine #2, I shared the many strategies and struggles I'd been through with my 3 children, and gave her some advice on what had worked best for us.

A week or so later, I ran into my sister-in-law at the supermarket. Shopping for diapers for my niece. She too shared that potty training her daughter was turning out to be much more of a nightmare than she'd anticipated.

By now, something was pinging in the back of my mind. All parents had to potty-train their kids, right? And in the space of two weeks I'd run into two who were having trouble with it.

I know the hardships that came with it, especially being a working parent. I understood the sheer terror that gripped potty-training parents sometimes, and the irrational fears that poked at their minds.

That evening, I sat down and wrote up some notes. What had I done that had worked well? How did potty training my boys differ from potty training my daughter? Was there anything that definitively **had not** worked? How did my daughter learn in such a short period of time? By the time I went to bed, I had a mini-manual to share with the two women in my life who were struggling with this milestone.

What you're reading right now is a more comprehensive, fleshed-out, beefed-up, value-added version of that first potty-training blueprint, that's aimed specifically at potty training boys.

As you work your way through this book, you'll learn:

- How to know when your child is ready for potty training
- The myths about potty training and what to believe instead
- How to avoid common potty-training mistakes
- What the 3-day method is all about
- How to set yourself (and your child) up for success
- How to deal with regressions
- The best ways to make potty training stick

This book is **not** a one-size-fits-all kind of thing. While I can guarantee that these methods, tips, and tricks will work for 80% of children, you understand your child best. Some things will work exceptionally well with your kids. Others won't. That's normal, and you'll need to take the fundamentals that you learn here and adapt them to suit your kids.

I can tell you that you'll put this down with a much better knowledge of potty training and all it entails, and it will do wonders for boosting your confidence right from the beginning of the process. Don't underestimate the power of confidence! An unconfident parent makes for an anxious child. You can do this, and so can your child!

So, what makes this the book for you? I can hear you saying "But there are hundreds of potty training books out there, what makes this one different?" Well, this one will teach you all you need to know to get your child toilet trained - in less time than it will probably take you to read it.

Time is of the essence! Nobody wants to spend months doing something (especially something involving bodily fluids and poop) when you *could* spend a week.

Teaching your child to use the toilet is much easier than it may seem at this moment. Trust me. I've done it three times over, and I'm here to tell you it's easier than you think!

So why don't all parents get it right immediately?

The Problem

When I was around potty-training age, my mother was a stay-at-home mom. My father would leave the house early every morning to take a train to work, and arrive back in the evenings. Mum would get us kids out of bed, make us breakfast, and keep a watchful eye on us playing as she cleaned the house. She'd put us down for naps and make a home-cooked meal for my father, so he could eat immediately when he arrived home.

When it came to potty-training me and my siblings, she didn't have blueprints and guidelines and books. What she did have, though, was **time**.

In between cleaning and cooking, she had hours to spend with us. She had the time and space to get creative with teaching us, and it was all done over a period of time.

In today's world, many moms work just as long hours as dads do. Children spend more time at daycare than they used to, and let me assure you that nobody at daycare is going to make the effort to potty-train your child while you're at work!

Parents these days just *don't have enough time* to potty-train kids (Bureau of Labor, 2020). What usually happens (and we're all guilty of it) is that we make a good start on a Saturday morning, Sunday goes well, Monday is decent, and we have a bad day on Tuesday so things fall by the wayside. On Wednesday, we do half a job at potty training, and on Thursday night we decide we'll pick it up on the weekend again.

Inconsistency is one of potty training's biggest enemies. Just like with anything, if we want to become good at it (or teach our kids to be good at it), we need to work at it consistently.

Parents' working schedules are one of the biggest and most common problems when it comes to effectively potty training kids.

The Solution

If you could come home on Friday night to a child wearing diapers and leave for work on Tuesday morning with an almost completely fully potty-trained child, would you do it?

If it required some preparation and some work from you over the weekend, would you sacrifice some of your time to potty-train your child once and for all?

The 3-day method is **the perfect way** for busy working parents to toilet train their child effectively.

There's no need to worry about enduring months of working through this stage of your kid's life. Whether this is your first time, or you've already been through it with a couple of kids already, the 3-day method is highly effective.

With the proper follow-up, some patience, and a whole lot of support and encouragement, your child should go from baby to little big person in just a weekend!

About Stephany Hicks

Who is Stephany Hicks? Well, I'm a mom of three (2 boys and a girl, who are college-aged now!)

That means I've been through the "potty-training your child" stage three times. I discovered that each one of my children responded differently, so I spent hours trying out every method and technique I could find.

I've not only managed to potty-train my own children effectively, but I've been fortunate enough to have been in the position to give countless folk advice on doing the same quickly and effectively. When you've been through the process three times, each with different paths but the same results, you have a pretty good idea of the feelings, issues, and worries that come along with it!

Helping you matters to me. It took me three tries to learn how to go through the process in an effective way that was fairly free of stress - for **both** parent and child.

I'm all about making this process easier on parents. The stresses that can come with it can be brutal and spill over into other areas of life. But a huge part of the reason behind this book is to make this process easy **on your child too**.

Remember, your tyke is at an age where they're learning. Unnecessary stress can lead to toxic behaviors from parents, such as punishing your child in public or inadvertently embarrassing them. Reaching this milestone shouldn't be such a huge and scary thing!

I've written this book to share my passion for helping other parents find balance in their lives, and the lives of their kids.

This doesn't have to be difficult. It will certainly require some work and some time, but the mission is to make it easy for everyone involved. Don't just take my word for it, though! Let's get right into chapter one.

Chapter 1:

Taking the First Step

"If you want your children to turn out well, spend twice as much time with them, and half as much money." - Abigail Van Buren

The above saying is one of my favorite quotes. As a mother, I sometimes worried that I spent *too much* time with my kids and didn't let them have as much freedom as others. But as my children have grown and gone off to college, I can look back and see the value in how much time we spent with our kids, and not how much money we spent on them.

Don't get me wrong - your child needs decent clothes, shoes, school supplies, food, and so on. But spending money on your children will never have the same effect (on them or on you) as **spending time** with them does.

This is true for every aspect of your child's life, potty training included. You can't pay anyone to potty-train your child for you - you need to put in the time *yourself*. The fact that you're reading this right now is a great start, and is the first step on the road to toilet training your child effectively, while learning a few things (about them and yourself) along the way.

If you think about it, you're the *ideal person* to potty-train your son. You've been with him since he was born - you know him best, by far. The success of his potty training depends largely on you!

There's no need to feel any pressure, though. It's just important to understand that if potty training isn't working, it's not your son's fault. It just means that you haven't figured out what works for him. You'll need patience and perseverance to get it right, and don't be afraid to change things up if something isn't working for you or him.

The 3-day method is a baseline, a foundation. What you build on it is up to you. The principles and techniques in this method are highly effective, but they'll never be as effective as they could be if you aren't tailoring them to your individual child.

Yes, potty training is like any other training! You can customize it as much as you want while remaining within the basic foundations. And we all know kids - if something is of interest to them, they'll learn it a whole lot faster than if they aren't really that excited by it.

Let's start at the very beginning. The first thing most parents struggle with is when to start toilet training their child. In this chapter, we'll discuss the signs to keep an eye out for that show that your child is ready to be taught.

We'll give you a brief outline of how the 3-day method works and why you should use it over other training techniques. We'll end with a checklist of things you'll need for your 3-day training so you can prepare well. Good preparation is half the battle won!

By the end of chapter 1, you'll know when your boy is ready, and you'll be ready too.

How Do I Know My Son is Ready for Toilet Training?

At some point, all parents get tired of diapers. They cost a chunk, changing them takes time out of your day, and of course, there's the poop-handling thing. Every parent *will* get poop on them at least a few times.

As soon as your child begins to start looking and acting like a real little adult person (i.e. being opinionated, strutting around confidently, and enjoying watching you being hit with something), it can be extremely tempting to leap right in and start trying to get the potty training underway.

Woah! Hold up. Just because you're ready to stop handling your kid's excretions, doesn't mean they're ready to move to a big person's toilet.

Although there is no specific age at which children should be potty-trained, jumping into it too early can lead to much more frustration down the line, for both parents and the child.

If you do a bit of research on the internet or ask friends and family how old their kids were when they potty-trained them, you're likely to get a rather large variety of different answers. 14 months, 18 months, 3 years…This is as random as how quickly a child's hair grows, or when they get hungry.

Most children begin learning to use the toilet between 18 months and 3 years of age (Choby & George, 2008)5. That's quite a large range, though, and there's no telling where your kid will fall on the scale. Just because your sister's children both started at 18 months, that doesn't mean your kid will be ready at the same age. It's personal!

At the same time, though, you don't want to be blind to your child's needs and leave them in diapers until way past all their friends have been potty-trained. It can be a source of frustration and worry for parents who aren't sure **when** to start toilet training, never mind how!

The good news is that our little ones are smarter than we give them credit for. When your son is ready to begin potty training, he'll display some signs that you should be looking out for.

Once you spot two or more of these signs, and they're consistent (he does them more than once), you'll know your little tyke is ready to be trained in the ways of big people.

Indicators to Look Out For

Humans are amazing creatures. Our bodies are built to be serious machines that run almost automatically. The link between the body and the brain is even more fascinating, especially when you have a child.

As he grows, you'll notice those moments when something "clicks," or when he's examining an object with an interest and focus that most of us adults don't even have.

When your son is ready, he'll give you some indicators that potty training should commence. Bear in mind that this doesn't mean he *knows* he needs to be potty-trained. It's a natural progression that he won't understand, but it's important to pay attention to his behavior so you don't miss these signs when they come.

- **Showing Related Interests**

You may be wondering what a "toilet-related interest" is! All this means is that your son will start showing an elevated interest in the potty or toilet and things that go with it.

For example, he may give you an indication that he wants to wear " big-boy underwear" instead of a diaper. He may ask questions about the toilet or potty. He might even want to watch other people go to the toilet, out of curiosity.

Don't think it's weird if your little boy is showing an interest in watching you or his dad do your thing in the bathroom. Like everything, he first gets the inkling of how to do this by watching and learning from his parents.

Be open with your son. He's learning many things, and wanting to observe is simply a part of his knowledge journey.

Of course, if he starts following strangers into bathrooms or makes other people uncomfortable by staring at them while they're on the toilet, then it's time to have a bit of a chat.

But him wanting to watch his parents or siblings is natural. He also may have questions about why mom and dad do things differently. It's important to be open and at no point should you ever make him feel bad for being curious (as long as it's within the boundaries I mentioned above).

- **He's Becoming Uncomfortable in Diapers**

Be careful not to jump the gun on this one and make the decision for your child. But you should be aware of the signs that he's getting uncomfortable in diapers and would be better off without them.

The biggest sign of this is your son wriggling out of his diaper on the playground or in the bathroom (it can be rather shocking when you know you sent him to daycare with a diaper, and he comes back without one!), or if he complains to you about wet or dirty diapers.

Coming back from the playground with a skew diaper doesn't qualify! Just because he's playing rougher now and the diaper isn't quite staying where it should be, it doesn't mean he's ready to go without one.

I can't stress enough that you *should not* decide that he's uncomfortable based on what you see. The hanging, leaky diaper may make *you* uncomfortable, but he might not even notice it yet!

The best thing you can do is wait. Push through those moments that make you wonder "How does he not feel that?" and let your child work this out on his own. Understanding when he's not comfy and being able to verbalize that is also a huge part of his development.

If he complains to you about his diaper being wet, smelly, or uncomfortable, then that's a sure sign that he's ready to be rid of them!

- **He Expresses the Need to Go**

If your little boy understands his own body well enough to know when he needs to go, that's another big sign that it's time to start the training.

Babies start off with a complete lack of control over their bodily functions. For their first year or two, they don't have to even think about it. They simply wear a diaper and mom and dad take care of the rest.

Their senses are not yet developed enough to understand when they need to go, and even if they were, they wouldn't be able to tell us yet! But as your child grows, they begin to become more aware of their own bodies and physical feelings.

They'll also start to realize what feeling leads to what outcome. They may not be able to explain that nagging feeling in their bladder, but they know it leads to a wet diaper! As their senses develop, they'll also begin to feel more and more discomfort when their diaper is wet or dirty.

This is when they'll begin telling you that they need to go. Keep in mind that "telling" won't always mean verbally. Some children can speak enough at this stage to convey their wishes, but others can't yet.

If your child isn't at the point where he can tell you verbally that he needs to go to the toilet, he'll start showing you instead. Body language is extremely telling. If he's squatting in a strange way, grabbing at his groin area, or covering his bum, those could quite well be him telling you he's ready to take the next step.

- **He's Physically Able To**

Just like with potty training, there's no right or wrong age for babies to start doing things like walking, running, balancing, and so on. Motor skills develop differently in each child, and that's completely normal.

It stands to reason that if your child is not yet physically developed enough to hold himself up while sitting on a potty or not coordinated enough to get it right, he's probably not ready for toilet training.

Rushing your little boy into this when he's not physically able to support himself can have some disastrous consequences. Potty training shouldn't be something that can lead to injury!

You also don't want to get your little one in the habit of needing your help to get on or off the potty. From the start, this needs to be about independence as much as about comfort and hygiene!

For these reasons, I highly recommend waiting until your son can do this on his own before attempting to potty-train. If you need to wait a bit longer than other parents, so be it!

You may need to practice sitting down on a potty and getting up before you get into the actual training. When he's able to do both of those actions by himself without any help from mom or dad, then he's physically ready to be taught how to use the potty.

- **His Diaper Stays Dry for 2+ Hours**

As babies grow into toddlers, their body becomes smarter at doing things. He might not be consciously trying to hold it in because he wants to play longer. But the body gets stronger and better at controlling itself, leading to fewer "accidents."

Of course, as he grows his body will also be getting bigger physically. That means more capacity for storing physical waste, so it takes longer before he actually needs to go to the bathroom.

As he's growing, his senses are developing too. The combination of more physical space and a more developed body and brain connection means that he doesn't need to go as often as he used to.

If your little boy's diaper stays dry for 2 or more hours and doesn't need to be changed, it could be a sign that he's just about ready to move on to the training stage.

Again, be careful with this. If you notice his diaper has been dry for 2 hours today, don't rush to start potty training tonight. Consistency is important. You'll need to see a 2-hours-plus dry diaper on multiple days before you can safely assume that it's time for the next step.

Also, bear in mind that this needs to happen when he's with you and you can observe him. If you dropped him off at daycare with a dry diaper and returned four hours later, and he still has a dry diaper, you can't assume that he's been in the same dry diaper for four hours. Chances are one of the daycare staff has changed his diaper sometime during the day.

You'll need to actively monitor him when he's at home in order to be sure that he really is going 2 hours or more without wetting his diaper.

- **He Has a Poop Schedule**

Pooping on a regular schedule is another hint that your son may be just about ready to learn to use the toilet. This can be difficult to monitor, though, unless he immediately tells you that he needs a diaper change (and we've already covered this above - if he's telling you he needs to be changed, he's probably ready).

If you have a regular changing schedule and you notice that he seems to poop at roughly the same time every day, it's a good sign that his body is doing things as it should and developing well.

He's definitely on the path to learning how to use the potty. But make sure not to take this sign on its own as an indication that you should start toilet training.

Pooping habits can be affected by a number of things. Perhaps the daycare has started feeding the kids guava with their lunch, and your little tyke's tummy doesn't like it too much. He's pooping right on schedule 30 minutes after lunch, but it's not because his body is creating its own routine - it's because it's just trying to get rid of the guava!

If you do spot this sign, make sure that it comes in conjunction with other signs, and not on its own. It's another sign that works better when you're around your kid the whole day and know exactly what he's had to eat and drink, so you're sure it's not just his body trying to expel something it doesn't agree with.

- **He Can Follow Basic One-Step Instructions**

Although you won't be able to explain the mechanics of peeing and pooping to a child (and why would you want to, really?) there needs to be a certain level of communication in order for him to learn how to go to the toilet on his own.

He needs to be able to understand the difference between "potty terminology" like "pee" and "poop." He needs to understand what's actually going on, and be a willing participant, not be dragged along through something he doesn't understand or want to be doing.

And he needs to be able to follow instructions. I'm not talking about trying to make sense of a microwave user manual. I mean a simple, one-step instruction from his mom or dad. Remember, you need to teach your little guy, and as much as he learns from watching and copying, sometimes that's not quite enough.

Consider your son watching how his mom does it and then wanting to sit down every time he tries to pee. Some things need explaining along with the example. He needs to be able to take instruction from you, so he can do the right thing every time.

Even when he's got the method down, there are things that you'll need to reinforce, such as flushing the toilet and washing hands. These are best reinforced verbally. There's no point in you flushing the toilet after him to lead by example. Then there's nothing left for him to flush!

If you've spotted more than one of these signs, and they've been around fairly consistently, you can safely assume that your little boy is ready to take the next step!

All that remains is to figure out how to teach your tyke this thing that we do every single day without giving it a second thought. You'll know by now that there are many methods and everyone has their own preferences, ideas, and tips for imparting this knowledge and habit onto your kiddie.

But I know - you know your child best. Which is why I'm giving you this 3-day blueprint as a foundation, so you can tweak it and build on it to cater for your child. Each child is unique!

You may be wondering if 3 days is enough to teach your toddler this important life skill. It may sound too good to be true! Rest assured; it's both true and enough time. Here's why you've chosen wisely in investing in this book and training method.

Why Choose the 3-Day Method?

As much as we parents look forward to the day we no longer have to change diapers, we also secretly dread our babies growing up and becoming little big people themselves. But potty training must be done, and I can guarantee that it will be far less painful to push through 3 tough days than to drag it out over 3 or 4 months.

Every parent you chat to will have their own thoughts and opinions on the "right approach" to toilet training kids. Remember, every kid is different! Their child may have responded really well to one particular thing, but there's no saying your son will have the same response!

Mention 3-day potty training, and many people will give you a sideways look. You may get an incredulous laugh or two. Some may scoff, others may raise an eyebrow, and yet others may look on you with pity at the thought of such a ridiculous time frame.

I say this upfront and with much passion - DO NOT let others' scoffs and contrary advice make you feel like a silly parent. I can tell you with absolute confidence that the 3-day method works - I've done it myself, with my third child.

It worked so effectively for me that I've passed it on to every parent I know going through potty training, and many of them (at least 80%) have had the same results as I have.

Regardless of what others think, here are a few reasons the 3-day method is such a good one.

It Doesn't Interfere Much With Schedules

Modern parents have less time to spend on potty training than our parents and our parents' parents did. That's just the way today's world works - often, both parents have full-time jobs and spend fewer hours with their children than parents once did.

This is no criticism - it's a normal thing. Potty training can become more complicated when mom and dad's schedules are different, or when they work long hours. Nobody wants to come home and work on potty training every night before bed!

The 3-day method can be done over a long weekend, or at the cost of a day's leave from work. It's not much of a sacrifice to teach your child how to use the toilet effectively!

It Minimizes Frustration

For both parents and children. I'm not saying the 3 days will be devoid of frustration - there will definitely be moments. But a few frustrating experiences over the course of 3 days far outweighs multiple frustrations over 3 months.

And if you're finding potty training frustrating and draining, imagine how your little boy must feel! Remember, kids are much more sensitive to feelings than we realize. Every time you get annoyed or frustrated, he may not be able to understand, but he can sure feel it.

Getting potty training over and done with in a 3-day blitz means your little boy won't be spending months feeling like he's done something wrong. You may not realize it or intend for it to happen, but considering kids' self-esteem and beliefs about themselves are most malleable before the age of 7, something as simple as a drawn-out, frustrating toilet training experience can have long-term effects.

It Avoids Subjecting Your Child To Conflicting Training

If you're trying to toilet train your child but you only see them for an hour a day and on weekends, it's entirely possible that they may be more influenced by other adults they spend more time with.

Daycare staff, although they generally do not get involved in potty training, may take it upon themselves to do so if they feel it's necessary. In the same vein, if your child has a nanny, it may seem like a natural thing for them to help transition when the child is ready.

The downside is that your child may be getting two different methods from two different people. When you get home in the evening and take the opportunity to spend some time working with your child on it, you may be doing the opposite to what they're being told during the day.

Getting it over and done with in one weekend means no external influences to confuse matters. From there, it's just a case of constant reinforcement, and if necessary, sitting down with the nanny to make sure she's on the same page as you!

What is Needed to Use the 3-Day Method?

You'll need to prepare beforehand in order for the 3-day method to be the most effective. Thankfully there's not a lot of prep to do, and it will be well worth it!

Understand that you don't *need* to go out and get every single thing I mention here. This is a basic "potty training kit," but feel free to customize it to suit you, your child, and your family.

But I do recommend trying to stick to these things as closely as you can. Leaving one thing out because you don't think you'll need it will diminish the results.

For example, if you don't believe in rewarding your child with snacks or toys, that's completely fine. I'm not suggesting you should break core beliefs here - simply swap candy and toys out for something your child would be responsive to, such as a visit to a friend.

We'll go through some alternatives as we get into more detail about each step later on in the book, but it's important to stick to each step as closely as possible for optimal results!

Here are the things you'll need to be able to make the most of this approach and really get great results.

3 Full Days of the Parents' Time

When I say "full days," I mean *full* days. I don't recommend trying to do this over a weekend where you've committed to going to a barbecue with friends, planned to meet someone for coffee, or your other kids have stuff going on.

I understand that you can't just stop life for 3 days, though! But I recommend:

- Trying to get any other kids out the house for the weekend.
- Making alternate arrangements for fetching or picking up other children.
- Making and freezing/refrigerating meals in advance.
- Letting the important people know that you'll be unavailable for socializing.

- Planning some activities in advance for your little potty-trainer to prevent boredom and frustration.
- Ensuring you and your spouse are on the same page about how the weekend is going to happen!

I can't stress this point enough. A half-hearted attempt at the 3-day method *won't* work. You won't be doing anything intense or crazy, don't worry. But it is essential that you're available at any time during these three days to make the most of **every opportunity** to teach your little one how to do this right.

Would you rather spend an hour every night and the days on weekends for three or four months trying to train your kiddie, or simply commit to 3 full days? It's a no-brainer, really!

Remember that your kiddie needs to be kept busy and stimulated as the weekend goes. You'll be doing your training, but it's fairly subtle, and they should be just going about their weekend as they would normally. Make sure you've organized some stuff to keep them busy so you don't run into a sticky situation!

The Right Mindset

The effectiveness of the 3-day method depends most of all on *you*, not your child! Your mindset can make or break the success of this potty training mission.

Your child will take their cues from you. If you're annoyed, grumpy that your time has been disrupted, and impatient, he'll feel it. Don't underestimate how sensitive children are to these things!

You need to go into this weekend excited, ready for great things, and full of optimism. Even if your child isn't aware of all the preparation that's gone into it, he'll pick up on your enthusiasm about it and feel comfortable, happy, and in exactly the right frame of mind to be very teachable.

Be very mindful of this as the weekend goes on! You'll need to be conscious of how you're coming across to your child. Make sure you:

- Stay calm, no matter what happens.
- Be patient! Things *will* happen.
- Praise your child when he does it right.
- Be positive, even if you're feeling frustrated.
- Be consistent! If you're inconsistent, you may end up having to redo the whole experience.

A Potty Chair or Add-on Seat

If you've potty-trained other kids before this one, you may have one of these lying around or stashed in a garage somewhere. If not, you'll have to buy one.

There are two types of potties:

- **A freestanding potty chair**

These "mini toilets" are not only cute, but they also give your toddler his very own toilet. This is great for little ones who take pride in their own possessions.

It's basically a kiddie-sized toilet, which makes it super easy to use and not as intimidating as the grown-up toilet. This is a fantastic option for kids who show some fear at the idea of the toilet.

There's no water in it, so they don't need to worry about falling in or getting wet. It's also the perfect height for your little one to sit down on and stand right up again.

The downside? You'll need to empty your toddler's waste into the big toilet, flush it down, and clean the potty chair. But it's no worse than changing a diaper, so there's nothing to worry about!

- **A kiddie-sized seat attachment for the big toilet**

This is a small toilet-seat type attachment that fits over the regular seat to create an opening the appropriate size for a toddler. Some toddlers will love this as it's exactly like what mom and dad are doing.

It's very light and easy to take with you out in public or when visiting others. There's also no need for cleaning up afterwards. This is a great training aid to remind your little one to flush!

You'll need a little step for your son to stand on, so he can reach the toilet. Make sure you're right beside him when he uses it, so he can gain confidence with the height.

It's actually a pretty good idea to buy both. Start off with the potty chair, and move to the attachment once your son is confident enough for the big toilet. If you need to shop for a product, I recommend taking your little boy with and letting him help you choose. He'll be so excited it will be like getting a new toy!

Note that you need to have purchased your potty **before** the weekend. It needs to be ready and waiting for training.

New Underpants

Getting rid of diapers means your child will need something to wear under his pants! Again, you'll need to buy these before the weekend. This is another thing you can get your son excited about! Take him with you when you shop, and let him choose some of his own.

I advise getting 20 to 30 pairs. I know, you may be wondering why you need so many. Well, there are bound to be accidents, and you don't want your boy to have to go pantless while he waits for them to be washed.

Rewards

While bribery is never the best way to get things done, it's a useful little way of reinforcing lessons!

Depending on what you feel comfortable with, you can:

- Use your son's favorite snacks.
- Get some new, small toys.
- Create a chart and give reward stickers.
- Choose "experience" rewards - for example, a visit with a friend, a trip to the zoo, etc.

Keep a stash of stuff handy for the weekend. If you're using experience rewards, create some sort of system to keep track of what he's earned.

The Right Diet

Of course, any meal or drink will eventually lead to toilet time. But for this weekend to be most effective, you want to be feeding your kiddie high-fiber foods and snacks, and plenty of beverages.

Basically, we're aiming to get your little boy to recognize when he needs to go (which should be often considering the fiber and liquid intake), and to do it the right way.

Three, two, one...

Once you've set the dates, taken leave if you need to, made sure your schedule is clear, and ticked all the preparation boxes, you're ready to begin!

How Will This Book Help You?

Don't forget to keep this book by your side as you go through this process. It will:

- Walk you through each day in detail.
- Offer tips and tricks to adapt to your toddler's needs.
- Give solutions to common problems parents face.

Before we get straight into the program, we're going to tackle some of the misconceptions about potty training that may be a worry for parents.

Image by PublicDomainPictures from Pixabay

Chapter 2:

Potty Training Myths and Misconceptions

Potty training, as a parent, is kind of like going to the gym. If you haven't done it before, just the idea of it can be quite intimidating. It may seem like everyone else there knows exactly what they're doing, and there you are, floundering around. It can feel like all eyes are on you, and everyone knows that you're a fake!

In reality, everyone there is doing their own thing. You can eyeball the buff guy in the corner and do what he's doing, but you may not be able to keep up. You could sneak a peek at the slim girl who's been running on the treadmill for an hour and copy her, but you may hate every minute of it.

In the same way, every parent has their own idea of what works best. What's worked for one may have been an epic fail for another. There is no right or wrong for all! It's a very personal thing, and it's not even actually about *you*. It's about your child, and what really works for **them**.

If you *really* want to be confused about what works and what doesn't, Google how to potty-train your toddler. There's a ton of information online, but the majority of it is not what I'd consider healthy! You'll find everything from locking your child in a bathroom to having a religious ceremony. Yes, there's some ridiculous stuff out there!

Some of it sounds great, though. Especially those methods and techniques that have plenty of successful parents raving about them. They're worth a try if you really find something that speaks to you, but why try it on its own? Why not take techniques that appeal to you and incorporate them into your 3-day method for maximum efficiency?

Whether you're a first-time potty training parent or revisiting the process, it may be a little overwhelming to try and delve through the info that's out there. This chapter is dedicated to the common myths and misconceptions that many parents encounter while trying to train their children.

We'll discuss the inaccuracies, the physiological backing behind these things, why they've become such popular beliefs, and why there's absolutely no need for you to worry about them.

Let's dive into the world of potty training myths!

Common Myths

If you *want* to feel like a terrible parent, Google is the best way to get you there. There's a ton of wildly inaccurate information out there, and the worst thing is that just because it worked for some, it's taken as the gospel truth.

Google is not your best source of information here! You know what is? Your own knowledge of your child, plus a bit of common sense.

If you decide to do a little research (and let's face it, who won't?) there are some statements, techniques, and methods that you'll most likely come across that might seem a little…weird.

Some of them are downright ridiculous, but some of them have just enough merit to seem logical at first glance. So how do you know what's worth trying and what's not?

We're going to cover some of the most common myths about toilet training, why they're ridiculous (or not ridiculous, but still incorrect), and dispel them based on science, psychology, and logic about the human body.

Then, we'll cover some universal truths about toilet training your child. Having a better understanding of what information is false and what's true will get you off to a good start on your family's potty training journey.

Remember, not all of these are utterly ridiculous and impossible. Some of them work for some parents, otherwise they wouldn't be out there as legitimate ways to do this! But while they may work, the lasting effects they can have on a child aren't always a good thing.

It's up to you what you decide to do for your child. We will go through the 3-day method in detail from the next chapter, but if you find something of value here that you feel would be worth adding to the 3-day training, by all means, do so.

I'm not here to tell you that one thing works and one thing doesn't. Every one of these methods or ideas *can* work. But they're honestly not the right thing for every child. In fact, many of them will only work with a very specific type of child.

With that in mind, let's get right into it! Here are some common misconceptions about training your child to use the toilet.

You Should Ask Your Son Often If He Needs to Go

Have you ever been on a road trip with your kids? It's great for the first few hours, when they're excited about heading off, then they settle in with a book or a game, then they get excited again when the scenery starts to change.

But inevitably, after 5 hours of driving you'll hear "Are we there yet? When are we stopping? How much longer?" and a variety of other complaints that just go on, and on…and on.

You know how annoying that is, and how much you want to whip around and yell, "Be quiet. I'll tell you when we're there!"

Now imagine being in your child's shoes and constantly being asked "Do you need to go? Do you need to pee? Is it bathroom time? Do you think you need to poop?" And so on...and on.

Eventually, your little boy is going to think there's something wrong with him if he *doesn't* need to go! Treating your child in this way not only indicates a lack of confidence in him being able to verbalize when he needs to go, but it also means that he will most likely start to associate the toilet with pressure.

There's a school of thought that if you get your child thinking about whether or not they need to go every five minutes, it will become second nature to them to know when they do or when they don't. The problem with this idea is that asking your child *if* they need to go is doing nothing to get their physiological processes going.

Remember, your child is still developing. There's a physiological process that happens between the body and the brain when a person needs to relieve themselves. But we aren't born with it - it develops along the way (National Center for Biotechnology Information, 2019).

Your son needs to start listening to his body. This is something *you* can't teach. It happens naturally, when the body and brain communicate. Can you remember when you learned how to tell if you needed to pee? Of course not. It happens without us thinking about it.

If you're constantly bombarding him with questions about whether or not he needs to go, the only thing that's happening is he's feeling pressured to need to go. There's a possibility that he'll start to become hyper-vigilant and decide that he needs to go when he actually doesn't, because he feels like he ***should***.

This can lead to plenty of frustration. Parents will think the baby is taking a step forward, and be disappointed when they get to the toilet and have nothing to do. Baby will feel like they *should* have something to do, and be mortified when they get to the toilet and nothing happens.

Bugging your child about it is not going to make them suddenly learn when they need to go. It could have negative consequences, instead of positive ones.

You Should Set a Timer to Have Your Child Go to the Bathroom Regularly

Some parents swear by a potty schedule. Simply set a timer for every hour, or half hour, or whatever suits you and take your kiddie off to the bathroom whenever the alarm rings.

Often, when parents notice their baby is pooping on a pretty regular schedule already (which is a sign of being ready to potty-train), they assume that this method is just a natural way of following on from that.

The danger here is similar to the myth above. You're putting pressure on your little one to pee or poop on a schedule that may not be right for their body. When the alarm rings and you take them to the toilet but nothing comes out, they're likely to feel embarrassed or ashamed.

This method is not really teaching children to associate the bathroom with needing to pee or poop. In a child's developing mind, all that's happening is that the bathroom is where they're *expected* to do this thing, at a certain time.

When they're constantly being marched to the toilet with the expectation of them peeing, it can lead to extreme anxiety. What if they don't need to go? Are they letting mom or dad down? Is something wrong with them? Do other kids pee every time the alarm clock goes off?

Do you see how this can come across in your child's mind? Remember, children don't think the same way we do. Their logic is flawed and not yet fully developed. All they know is that mom or dad keeps taking them somewhere and expecting them to do something they physically can't do.

This method can be damaging to children's psyche. While I'm sure most parents aren't going to admonish their child if they sit down but no poop appears, the constant feeling of expectation, letting their parents down, and defeat can be hard on a little mind.

There's also the possibility of your child feeling like they aren't allowed to go unless the clock has rung. This could lead to them holding it in when they really do need to go, because they're waiting for their "toilet time."

Instead of associating the bathroom with being the place to go when they feel the need to relieve themselves, they're creating an association with the alarm clock, or mom taking them by the hand to lead them to the toilet.

Imagine that instead of raising a child who knows their body and is confident in themselves, your child has to run to the bathroom every time they hear an alarm clock because their body is trained that way. Or the possibility of having an accident in class because they feel like they can't go when they need to, until they hear the bell ring for the end of class.

It may seem like a logical way to teach your child to use the toilet, but just a little digging exposes how some of the ways this could go wrong for your child.

If Your Child Tells You He Has Gone in His Diaper, He is Ready to Potty Train Right Away

It's a really good step for a child to be able to tell you when his diaper is wet or dirty. That means that he's aware of feeling discomfort and is starting to understand the difference between feeling dry and feeling wet.

Although we did cover this as one of the signs that your child is ready to begin potty training, remember that it needs to come with other signs, not as a standalone thing.

Being aware that they *have* gone is **not** the same thing as being aware that they *need to* go.

It's kind of like taking a drive to a destination you're a little unsure of. You may not realize it at the moment that you've just taken a wrong turn. You certainly won't know in advance that you're going to take the wrong turn. But it won't take long for you to realize that you're lost.

Knowing you're lost is not the same as understanding the map well enough to not take the wrong turn in the first place.

If he's telling you often that his diaper is wet, or he wants to take it off, or it's getting uncomfortable, keep a careful eye out for other signs. If this is the only one, it's worth having a look at other reasons before going straight to potty training.

Some common reasons for children complaining about wet or dirty diapers include:

- Sensitive skin, especially in the diaper area.
- Getting caught on things as they play.
- Other children pointing it out.

If none of these are valid, but no other signs show up, give it a bit of time before deciding to start him on potty training immediately.

Rewards are Necessary for Effective Toilet Training

Another symptom of the modern world is that we tend to show love, caring, and praise by giving people stuff. It's especially true for our children! We buy them toys to make them happy and keep them busy. We get them the latest cool thing, so they can keep up with the trends. All of us parents are guilty of it—to some degree!

Of course, kids do need to be spoiled in some ways. They should eat well (so they can grow up healthy and strong and with an appreciation for good food), wear decent clothes (no need for brand names, but a proper fit is essential), and have the occasional treat that they love just because we adore them and want them to know it.

Remember the quote we began the book with? We should be spending more time and less money on our kids. In most cases, our children would be super happy with a hug, quality time, or a well-deserved praise. They don't always want a snack or a reward.

That doesn't mean you should never use candy, treats, or toys as rewards, though. They can be helpful for some children, and used as a bit of extra motivation when your child is struggling.

But you absolutely can potty-train your child without rewarding them for everything. Verbal reinforcement can be just as, if not more, effective than physical giving, when it comes to making lessons stick.

Don't get me wrong, you're allowed to spoil your child! I'm certainly not telling anyone how to (or not to) parent their child. I'm simply reinforcing the fact that while some kids will learn extremely quickly because they know they have a chocolate waiting for them, others will very soon get tired of chocolate and start feeling bored and disinterested.

Don't rely on rewards as a surefire way to get your child toilet trained. They're best used as a supplement to the 3-day training method. Do, however, be sure to lavish your child with love and praise when they get something right. That will do the trick far more than candy or games or toys.

Girls are Easier to Train Than Boys

As a mom who has been through potty training with two boys and a girl, I can tell you for sure that this isn't true in the slightest! There's absolutely no evidence to prove that one gender is harder to potty-train than the other.

Of course the mechanics are slightly different. Moms who have to teach boys may be unsure of how exactly to show them how to do their thing. Dads who have to teach girls may also struggle a little to teach their daughter in a relatable way.

But that doesn't mean that boys are harder to train, or girls are harder to train. If anything, the hardest kids to train are the stubborn ones - regardless of whether they're boys or girls!

Don't let anyone else's experiences cast a shadow on yours before you've even started. That woman on the potty training forum who swears that boys are a nightmare to train? Maybe her son is a little terror who walks all over his mother and knows how to get away with murder. Perhaps she's let him get away with anything he wants and now has a brat on her hands!

But the exact same can be true with girls. Boys aren't the only kids who become bratty. It all depends on how they've been raised, the respect with which they treat their parents (and with which their parents treat them), and the personality of the little tyke.

There's no such thing as "boys are harder to train than girls." Trust me, I've done both!

Your Son Will Tell You When He's Ready

As an adult, you can psych yourself up for anything. Got a doctor's appointment coming up? Do some calming breathing and prepare. About to play a sports match? Warm up on the field and get in the zone. Want to learn a new hobby? Choose when to start and how much time to dedicate to it.

Children are different, especially when they're still under the age of 10. They're developing and changing all the time. They're learning new things, about how to be, how to interact, and how *not* to do things.

Basically, they're just going with the flow, every hour, every day; surfing the waves of change. One day, they're just doing their thing, and the next day they've lost a tooth. Today they're all playing ball together and tomorrow they're suddenly aware that boys and girls are different.

It's quite a lot to take in as a kid. They don't know why things are happening to their body. In fact, most of the time they don't even know *how to describe* what things are happening. They just take it all in their stride and see where it leads.

So when it does come time for your child to learn how to use the toilet or potty, they're most likely not going to be able to tell you that. Your son has no idea of his anatomy, body terminology, or what exactly it is that he's feeling.

As adults, we know what it means when we feel that twinge in our bladder area. We know that when we drink too much coffee it can make our heart beat faster, or that going for a run in inadequate shoes will most likely result in sore feet later on. *We've learned.*

Your toddler hasn't learned. He doesn't even know that potty training is a thing, and if he did, he would have no idea how to prepare himself for it. How would he measure when he's ready? By physical development? By his state of mind?

While we adults can "get ready," your kid has no idea what that means, especially when it comes to being ready for a bodily process. That's like telling an adult to let you know when they're ready to learn how to ride an embedeezle. Yes. Exactly.

Your son will have absolutely no idea when he's ready to start learning how to use the big toilet. Even if he has an inkling of something, he's going to have no way of knowing how to communicate that with you.

Daycare Will Potty Train Your Child

Don't fall into the trap of assuming daycare staff will take care of this for you. It's understandable why many busy parents think this is something natural. After all, the staff see your kids more than you do sometimes!

But you wouldn't let the daycare staff discipline your child, would you? You wouldn't allow a virtual stranger to decide that something your child did was inappropriate and give them a smack on the bottom. That's not their call. They're not the parents.

So why do some parents feel that it should be up to this virtual stranger to teach your child one of the most intimate lessons they'll ever learn? It's not only robbing your child (and yourself) of valuable time together that could be spent bonding and learning, but it's also expecting far too much of someone whose responsibilities don't extend nearly that far.

In a practical sense, most daycare centers require children to be potty-trained before they're allowed to enroll anyway. On occasion, you will find one that assists with potty training, but this can sometimes cause more chaos and confusion than not.

If you're already teaching or guiding your child towards potty training, you may have a completely different approach than the daycare staff. It's confusing to a child to hear two different things, and have to change their behaviors to pacify each adult.

If you aren't potty training at all but instead expecting the daycare to do it for you, you may find your child coming home with habits you don't agree with or don't like, based on what someone else has taught them.

Also, the daycare may make use of a potty chair when all you have is a toilet trainer seat, in which case there's going to be some physical conflict with what your child is learning and what they're comfortable with.

You Should Not Let Your Child Wear Diapers Once They Start Toilet Training

Throwing the diapers away once and for all when you start potty training is a bad idea. I get it - sometimes you want that stage of life behind you, and it can also be a strong sign to your child that you truly believe they're going to nail this toilet training thing.

But it's always a good backup plan to keep them around for the foreseeable future, until you're *absolutely certain* they're not necessary anymore.

When you begin training your child, it may be necessary to put your child in a diaper at night. They may not be able to get out of bed and go to the bathroom themselves in the middle of the night, or they may have a nightmare and wet the bed.

Keeping the diaper on at night is a good safety measure for you and a confidence booster for your kid. If they're wearing their new underpants to bed, and they have an accident in the night, it could dash their confidence to the point where they regress.

Regression is another reality. This is when your child learns how to use the toilet effectively, but something causes them to take a step backwards again and lose their confidence or ability.

Of course, even if your child takes to the toilet like a bird to the sky, there's always episodes of upset tummies. Having a few diapers handy is always a good idea. Murphy's Law says you may never need them, but the moment you get rid of them entirely, you'll find a reason to need one!

Common Truths

Myths are everywhere, and it doesn't take much searching to find them.

It can be overwhelming to look at these myths. You start to think "There's so much to remember! What if I can't get this right? What if I mess up? What if I become the parent she's talking about in that one myth?"

Fear not, parent! The fact that you're worrying about that indicates that you have your child's best interests at heart!

But there's no need to become despondent reading through all those myths and misconceptions. Yes, potty training is a misunderstood process. But as much as there's a whole lot of false or half-story information out there, there are also certain universal truths when it comes to potty training your baby.

The good news is that these are as true as anything, and when you start to feel down or overwhelmed, come back to this page and read these again.

Every Child Is Unique

Your child is completely unique. His personality, his likes and dislikes, his fears and his joys. The way he learns is based upon these things, and so is the way he sees the world around him.

You don't have much control over the way your little one develops! What you do have control of is the way he learns to think of himself, how he learns to treat other people, and what he values in life.

You can't choose if he prefers beef or chicken. You can't decide for him that he should be a dog person. And you can't undo that strange fear he has of creepy crawlies. Some things are just built-in and developed along the way, without any input from you.

He's not going to like the same things as his sister. He's not necessarily going to want to play with the same toys as his friend. Your little guy has a mind of his own, and everything that comes in is filtered through it.

That means that just because one potty training technique worked for his sister, it won't necessarily work for him.

This isn't a bad thing! Remember, you know your little boy best. You know what he likes, what he responds to, and what it means when he has that expression on his face. You're totally at an advantage here, because you can cater this 3-day method to suit his very personality.

Uniqueness is not a bad thing when it comes to potty training. Whether you do it this way or that way, you're going to have to put in the work. But putting in the work is more enjoyable when you're slanting your work towards your little guy's likes and wants and needs.

You know him best, so you can adjust any program or technique to suit him and you. No need to follow what everyone is doing!

You're Not "Doing It Wrong"

There is no right or wrong way to do this. What's right for your friend's child could backfire horribly with your son. The method your sister scoffs at could end up being the one that does the trick for you.

Let me put your mind at ease. As long as there's no abuse of any kind, you're encouraging your child and treating him with love, and you have patience and trust in the process, there is **no way** you can get this wrong!

If anyone tells you that you're doing it wrong, it's your cue to find somewhere else to be. Don't let that sit around in your head, either. There are so many factors that go into successful potty training that nobody can say their way is the best.

I'll even go so far as to say that the 3-day method may not be for everybody. It's certainly not a magic fix, and there's no guarantee that your kid will never have an accident or regress.

If you look at this from the point of view of doing the best thing for your child, then you can't go wrong.

Moms Can Potty Train Boys (And Dads Can Potty Train Girls)

In some cases, moms may find themselves alone in their quest to potty-train their son, or dads may find they have to teach their daughter. It may be logical to assume that your child needs a parent of the same sex to potty rain them, but rest assured, this is not necessarily the case.

If you've already searched the internet for this, it can get wacky and ugly. Everybody has an opinion, but the reality is that these situations happen, and they're actually no different than a same-sex parent teaching their child.

Sure, some mechanics are a little different. A little girl may wonder why she can't stand and pee like her single dad does. A boy may struggle to aim properly because mom isn't sure how to teach him.

But these are things that can be remedied, and are certainly not enough to prevent effective potty training from happening. The 3-day method is suitable for all parents with any kids. There's no discrimination - I firmly believe that anybody can teach this to any child, with very few exceptions.

There Will Be Diaper Moments

We've already discussed this briefly, but it's definitely something you'll need to be prepared for. Diapers are going to happen, even after potty training is "finished."

Whether it's a nightmare that results in bed-wetting, anxiety or fear, an upset stomach, or simply distraction and not remembering to go, diaper moments are going to be around.

Don't think that you've failed if this happens. It's another perfectly normal and natural thing. Not every child will regress, and some may only need a diaper once in a blue moon.

Some, though, will take a step back completely and revert back to being fully reliant on diapers. There could be cause for concern behind this - there's often an underlying psychological or medical reason that needs to be dealt with before it can be fixed.

We'll discuss regression in a later chapter, but if your little one has the occasional diaper moment, there's absolutely nothing to worry about.

You <u>Can</u> Do This In Three Days!

Three days isn't much. It's the length of a long weekend, and we all know how fast those go when work is looming at the end of it. If you minus the hours we spend sleeping, it's even less time, really.

Perhaps you're not quite convinced that you'll get this right in just a weekend. Maybe your friends and family have shared their own horror stories with you, and you're wondering what your story will be when you get together again.

Well, I have good news. Your story will be about how you taught your child to use the big toilet in just one weekend. Your story will have a bit of frustration, a dash of humor, a lot of encouragement, and a triumphant ending.

If you put in the work, I can promise you'll get results within those three days.

Remember, you can't just drop it after those three days and assume that it's completely ingrained in your son's brain. You'll need to keep following up, reinforcing, and offering praise when he gets it right.

Yes, you *can* set the strongest foundation in just three days. All it needs is your time, your undivided attention, and your love for your son.

The next chapter is a guide to preparing for the big weekend. This should take place over about a month. That may sound like a whole lot of prep, but believe me, it's setting the stage for the best results.

Chapter 3:

Preparation

Whether you've potty-trained children before or this is your first time, preparation is key! Like so many things - taking a road trip, going in for surgery, moving house - proper preparation is essential to limit frustration, stress, and the chance of negative consequences.

Preparation for this epic potty training weekend falls into two categories: prepping the parents, and prepping the kiddie.

You know what's coming. You have the book, you'll be following specific steps, and you'll be in control when the weekend comes. Your spouse may be right on the same page as you. If they aren't, getting them there is part of the prep work.

Your child, on the other hand, is probably making mud pies right now without a care in the world. He has no idea that this weekend is being planned *just for him*. He doesn't know that you're planning on potty training, or that you've put aside all your plans, or that he's expected to take part in this weekend mission and come out of it minus diapers and wearing big-boy undies instead.

The poor little tyke may feel overwhelmed if he's thrown into the weekend with no preparation.

You've done all the hard work figuring out if your son is ready to be potty-trained or not. It is hard work, I know. It's not easy spying on your child and analyzing everything he does and says.

Did he just say 'go poop" or was that 'grape juice'? Is he staring at daddy because he's super interested in what he's doing by the toilet or is he distracted by the light bouncing off the tile? His hand kind of moved nearby his bum area, so is he telling me he has a dirty diaper?

I know it's not easy figuring out when your little guy is ready. There's also always a part of us that wants him to stay tiny and adorable forever and not grow up! But once you're sure he's ready, the next step is...Preparing him for what's to come.

Preparing Your Son

So your little dude has been displaying all of the signs that he's ready to move up to big-boy superhero underwear and use the toilet just like daddy. Congratulations! This is the first milestone *within* this bigger milestone - the starting point of a journey.

Your little guy is just going about his toddler life with no inkling of what his parents are going through at this realization. As far as he's concerned, nothing new has happened. While you and your partner are having in-depth discussions on toilet training and strategies and Googling the best potty to buy, he doesn't even know this is a thing.

So, it's only fair that you take some time to educate and prepare him before throwing him in the deep end with a three-day intensive potty-training retreat.

It's a good idea to schedule your 3-day weekend for at least a month in the future. That way, you have enough time to get your little boy educated, excited, and used to new things regarding potty training.

Here's how to get him ready for his potty-training camp.

Start Educating Him

Remember, although learning to pee and poop is completely natural, learning *where* to pee and poop is what's important here. That's not a natural thing to know. Once upon a time, back in caveman days, we went behind a tree and that was that. Maybe we buried it. Those things aren't true for today. While peeing and pooping is a natural behavior and **not** a taught one, doing it in the right place is definitely something you can teach.

When your little guy starts showing interest in toilet-related things, keep that interest going by starting your teaching immediately.

Let Him Observe

Whenever either parent or other family members need to go to the toilet, let your toddler follow and observe. Just be careful that he doesn't follow a complete stranger into the toilet to check him out, because that's just uncomfortable for everyone, not to mention the obvious safety aspect.

Although it's not necessary to have your son only follow dad into the toilet, it's a good idea to try and place a **bit more emphasis** on dad's toilet habits than mom's.

It may be beneficial to spend a week of your toddler *just* observing dad, before he goes with mom. It can be confusing for a little kid to see dad standing and mom sitting, then dad sitting. It may help get him used to things by letting him watch dad doing things both ways. That way, after a week or so when he observes mom, it's just a natural thing that he won't really question.

Potty training can be complicated enough - you may not want to have to explain the anatomical differences between a boy and girl right at this time too!

Encourage Curiosity

Openness is extremely important during this time. There's no place for shyness! This is your little guy, and he knows nothing rude or perverted yet. If he's craning his neck to check things out while you're wiping, don't turn away and cover up!

Allow him to look and ask questions if he has any. You may be surprised at what comes out of that little head of his! If your child is an early potty bloomer, he may not be able to word questions yet. If that's the case, just let him look and copy.

Never, and I repeat - NEVER - make your child feel embarrassed or ashamed for looking while you're peeing or pooping. This is a huge part of preparing your toddler for being toilet trained themselves. Remember, for the first few years of their lives, babies learn by mimicking their parents. This is just another thing he'll have to mimic to have the best chance of getting it right.

Play Aiming Games

While it's completely true that boys are no more difficult to potty-train than girls, you do have that issue of aim. Once a little girl is sitting on the potty or seat, there's pretty much nowhere the waste can go but where it should go. Boys, though... Well, that stuff can go everywhere.

At this stage of his life, your baby's motor skills are still developing. He may not be able to aim 100%. When we talk about accidents happening, they aren't always fully clothed accidents! Aiming accidents happen too.

It's a great idea to start implementing some aiming games in the month leading up to the potty training weekend. These don't have to be potty-related games. Something as simple as throwing a ball at a hoop or a target can improve your toddler's physical skills.

Play these games with your toddler as often as you can. Make it fun for him, and he won't even know he's having a potty training lesson! Praise him enthusiastically when he gets the ball in the hoop. You want him to *want* to get it in the right place.

Get Him Excited About It

Do what you can to get your little dude excited about learning toilet stuff. I know - how do you really make the toilet seem interesting and exciting?

If you're stuck for some inspiration, why not try:

- Placing brightly colored stickers on the toilet, toilet seat attachment, potty chair, or on the wall behind his potty chair.
- Get him a "toilet buddy," a fluffy toy that isn't allowed out of the bathroom.
- Create a sticker chart, and tell him you'll be using it very soon.

A surefire way of getting your toddler excited is to take him with you to purchase his very own potty chair and big-boy underpants.

Make an outing of it! Tell him that you're going to get him something special. It's probably a good idea to let him know what that is, because you really don't want him being disappointed when he's expecting a toy car, and he gets a potty!

Explain to him that you are going to get him his own special toilet and superhero underpants. Make a big deal of allowing him to choose up to 20 pairs. As mentioned previously, I advise you choose a few plain pairs too - up to 30 in total. That may sound like a lot, but believe me, they'll come in handy.

When you get home, he'll be rather upset if you stash it all away in the cupboard. But he'll only be wearing it properly from your potty training weekend. It's a good idea to let him choose one pair to keep with him in the meantime.

If he wants to wear it around the house, let him, but be prepared for accidents. If he just wants to keep it and look at it and sleep with it in the bed, let him do that too. It's basically a new toy that he got to choose, and it's a little reminder of all the others that are to come on his special weekend.

Try and stagger your preparation over the weeks leading up to the long weekend. Don't do all your shopping and encouraging and observing in one week and then let everything slide for the next three.

You need to keep this excitement going until the day finally arrives - the day he starts real, big-person training!

Parental Preparation

Although this experience is largely about your son, it's also about you. Don't get so busy preparing your son that you forget to prepare yourselves!

Some basic prep is essential in order for the weekend to go as smoothly as possible. Hiccups do happen, but the more organized this is, the less chance there is of emergencies happening. And let's be honest, nobody wants a hiccup when there's poop and pee involved.

I advise getting as much of this organized as soon as possible. That will give you a few weeks to make sure you're all set, and allow for plenty of time to get your little tyke excited about what's to come.

Schedule the Weekend

Plan the weekend in advance, just like you would a holiday. Choose which weekend suits you and your partner. Take time off work, if necessary. Make absolutely sure there's nothing to do and nowhere you need to go that weekend - no birthdays, no events, nothing. Make sure there's nothing going on for your son too! No school plays or sporting events, or classmates' birthday parties.

Pencil it into the calendar, with a red ring around it so you can't help but see it every day. You need to be quite aware of these dates, so you don't inadvertently book something on that weekend that you then need to go and cancel afterwards.

Inform Family & Friends

Once you've set the date, inform the important people in your life. This serves the dual purpose of letting them know long in advance that you're out of commission for that weekend, and also makes you accountable to someone!

Accountability is not necessary, but it's helpful. It also means you can't back out of your weekend at the last minute because you're just not feeling it. Procrastinating is never a good idea!

While I don't recommend pushing through a weekend if you're suffering from illness, a severe anxious or depressive episode, or a marital crisis, you certainly shouldn't be backing out just because you're "not ready." or because you're "just not in the right frame of mind."

Be accountable to someone, whether it's a family member or a close friend. They'll also be there to offer advice if you need someone to vent to!

Arrange for Other Kids to Spend the Weekend Out

If you have an older child who is already potty-trained, it could be a good idea to make arrangements for them to stay over at a friend's house, or perhaps spend the weekend with their grandparents.

I'm not saying you need to banish your other children from their own home just so the baby has his space. But it will certainly benefit you and your little one if he's the *only* distraction at home over this weekend.

You may need to put some work into making this seem like a really exciting event for your other kids too. Give them some ideas for what they'd like to do over the weekend, or who they'd like to spend it with.

It's highly important that you don't force other kids out of the house if they absolutely do not want to go. If they wish to stay home, you'll need to let them know that the baby is going to be learning to use the toilet, and they will need to be extra good.

You can get them involved if you'd like to - it could be a great way for them to feel involved and take some pride in being a big brother or sister. If they can't help, or they don't want to, that's okay too. It will just involve a bit more planning on your part and some careful coordination between you and your spouse to keep both kids busy while still training the little guy.

Go On a Potty-Themed Shopping Spree

We've already discussed this in a bit of detail above, as a way of getting your little boy excited about his potty training weekend that's coming up.

As covered briefly before, in order to do the 3-day method effectively, you'll need to buy:

- Potty chair
- Toilet seat attachment
- Big-boy underwear

If you've already been through this with one kid, it may be tempting to use the same potty chair. While I can see the practicality, I advise getting a new one. This will be something that your son chooses for himself, something that he forms an attachment to. His very own little toilet.

If you really can't get another, take some time to sit down with your little guy and customize the existing one. Finger paint, stickers, paper, and glue can be used to make your old potty chair a whole new creation. Let him draw what he wants, color what he wants, and add stickers to his heart's content.

An attachable toddler toilet seat is a bit different. Because it's actually part of the big toilet, there's a bit less possession going on with it (which is why I suggest getting both, even if you prefer the attachment - one is HIS). It's totally okay to use the one you used for your other children, as long as it's still strong and has no cracks or dents.

If you feel it would help, it could be worth buying more than one potty chair (or borrowing one or two more if you feel okay with that), so you can have one in the room with you, as well as in each bathroom.

Come Up With a "Well Done" Action

Young children don't always respond to verbal praise. Their brains are still developing, and sometimes they just don't understand what's going on. What they *do* understand are things that play off their five senses.

You know how we all have that baby voice that slips out when we're having a chat with an infant (or a dog, for that matter)? Well, it's not just a silly, goofy thing that babies bring out in us. Children understand tone of voice far easier than language. We're communicating in their way when we speak to them in our baby voice.

In the same vein, kids don't understand restraint when it comes to facial expression and emotions. They do understand body language, facial expressions, and gestures.

Because of this, I highly recommend sitting down with your partner and coming up with a funny action, dance, or sound that basically says "Well done! You're amazing!" just without words.

This could be:

- A dance.
- A funny action, like a nose boop.
- Sound can make it funnier! Choose something your kiddie can mimic.
- If your kid has a favorite song, incorporate it.

Now, whenever your child has a bit of success over the weekend, you're going to play that song on your phone and do your dance/action. If it gets your baby laughing, then you know you're on the right track!

You want it to be laughable and highly fun, so he learns quickly that he gets a dance/action and song if he does a certain thing.

Some parents may not be too comfortable with this. I understand! I was incredibly shy as a child, and it took me a very long time to get comfortable enough (even around my spouse and children) to let loose and do something like that.

If you aren't comfortable doing a dance, please don't feel like this step is useless for you. Get a squeaky toy from the store that makes a funny noise and use that as your "success cue." Get creative, but don't leave this step out.

Stock Up on Supplies

The goal for the weekend is basically to not have to leave the house, unless it's part of the training. You want to be able to give your child your full attention and make sure you don't miss anything.

You don't want to be spending an hour cooking and miss an accident. You also don't want to have to run to the store because you're out of milk. I advise creating a shopping list and making sure you have everything you could possibly need for three full days indoors.

Apart from your everyday groceries, I suggest making sure the following are organized the week before you do the training:

Meals

You'll want to be with your child as much as possible over these three days, so you don't want to have to be away for an hour or so preparing and cooking dinner. If you can, cook some extra meals during the week and freeze them for the three days' dinners.

Breakfasts and lunches could be simpler meals that don't need much preparing. All meals should be healthy, real food - the less processed food, the better (not only for your child's general health, but for their bowels, which is important when training them to poop in a potty).

Rather have too much food pre-prepared than too little. You can always eat another frozen meal the next week, but you don't want the panic of not having prepared food over the weekend.

It's also a good idea to have a food schedule for the weekend so you know exactly what you're eating when. This will take a bit of stress off, as well as give you an opportunity to see how your child's eating correlates to their toilet habits.

If you can, try to stick to high-fiber foods like:

- Oatmeal
- Whole grain bread
- Bran cereal

Snacks

Stock up on high-fiber snacks for your little guy to nosh during the day. The purpose of feeding him these specific snacks is to stimulate his digestive system and get things working down there. Fiber will also bulk up and soften the stool, making the whole pooping process much easier.

Kid-friendly high-fiber snacks to hide in the cupboard for the weekend include:

- Popcorn (be careful of kernels)
- Beans or legumes (fresh or dried)
- Dried fruit (especially prunes - but use in moderation)
- Most types of berries
- "Grainy" fruits like pears or apples
- Granola bars
- Grainy crackers

As with any snack, keep an eye on your toddler while they eat these, as many are small pieces of food that could pose a choking hazard.

You'll also need to be well stocked up with drinks. The more he drinks, the more he's going to need to pee! Watery snacks like watermelon or ice pops are also a really good idea.

Avoid sugary stuff as far as possible. Pure fruit juice is great as it contains a little fiber too. Water is the best option. If he doesn't like the taste, you can add a couple of drops of water flavoring. This is easy to find at local stores!

Cleaning Supplies

There *will* be accidents. Around the house. Cleaning supplies are going to be essential items over this weekend! You'll need to have these things close at hand (without seeming like you're waiting for your kid to pee on the floor):

- A plastic bucket
- Some cleaning rags
- A cleaning solution

You'll also need to keep a spare pair of underwear close by, and a towel or cloth to wipe your little guy down while changing him.

If you've ticked all these boxes, then let's forge ahead, shall we? The next chapter starts explaining day one of the process. I recommend reading it the night before you begin so you can get a proper head start. Remember, make sure you're stocked up on everything you need *before* the weekend starts!

Chapter 4:

Day One

So here we are, about to do this thing! You've set aside your whole long weekend to get this potty training thing done. You're ready and raring to go. By now, you should have:

- ❏ Freed up your entire weekend by cancelling or postponing any plans.
- ❏ Made arrangements for your other children.
- ❏ Cooked and frozen meals in advance.
- ❏ Created a mini schedule of activities to keep your son busy over the weekend.
- ❏ Invested in a potty chair or toilet seat, possibly both.
- ❏ Bought your son a stash of new big-boy underwear.
- ❏ Stocked up on liquids and high-fiber snacks.
- ❏ Had a discussion with your spouse so you're both on the same page.
- ❏ Let your family and friends know that you're unavailable except for emergencies.

If all the boxes are ticked, it's time to set things in motion.

This chapter is dedicated to day one of the process. We'll go through it in depth, explaining step-by-step what to do. This isn't set in stone, and if you fly through step one and two and your little tyke gets distracted because he's hungry, then by all means, have breakfast before moving on to step 3.

Just be sure to get all these steps in during the day. If you have time, you can repeat steps if you feel that it's important for your son to experience them twice. Apart from these steps, go about your day like normal, encouraging your son to do the same.

It's important that you try not to leave the house with your child during day one. Leaving will mean one of two things - either putting a diaper on, which you want to avoid, or leaving without a diaper and risking an accident that would be embarrassing for both you and your child and could start things off in a bad frame of mind.

I would like to emphasize the importance of taking this seriously. These steps have been designed for a reason. They're effective, but if you start leaving steps out or changing the process entirely, it could have negative consequences.

Yes, the process is customizable to an extent. Every child should feel comfortable and interested, but if you're removing steps in order to adapt to your child, that's defeating the point of this method, I'm afraid.

You can customize each step, for sure. Throw in something your little guy loves, and he's sure to be more interested. For example, if you're working on step 2, getting him excited about this process, you could put an extra pair of underwear on his teddy bear if it will get him excited. Show him how his favorite cartoon character wears underpants. Buy him a new action figure and call it Captain Big Boy Underwear. Whatever works, feel free to add it in to a step to enhance its effectiveness. Just don't skip or remove steps entirely.

Remember, you're the expert here! You understand his nuances, habits, and personality. Get creative! This doesn't have to be a boring, drawn-out experience for you. Have some fun with it!

- Take part in fun kiddie activities with your son. When last did you color a picture, build a Lego house, or kick a ball around the garden?

- Art projects are great for creative kids. Draw a picture of son and dad in their underwear. Design a pair of funky underwear. This passes the time and gets your boy excited about the topic.
- Have a chugging competition. One of the things we'll be emphasizing over the weekend is drinking a lot, so this could be a fun way of getting liquid in.
- A movie and high-fiber snacks is a great way to end each evening.

We'll go through day one step-by-step, explaining each one in detail. The instructions are straightforward and easy to follow, with no ifs, ands or buts! Simply fit these into your day.

I will also explain why each step is so important and why it's essential to do it and do it right. There will be some little advice nuggets throughout, which will usually be things I found to be game-changers or useful things to consider when I was doing the 3-day method myself.

Above all, remember that your attitude (and that of your spouse) is the biggest contributor to the success of this method! If you're excited, motivated, and determined to make this a good, successful weekend, then your little guy is going to be off to the best start.

If you're ill, in a foul mood, or impatient, I suggest you reschedule. Trying to train your little boy while you're in a bad way has the potential to have disastrous results.

Be calm (whatever happens), patient (as hard as it may be), and do your best to make this fun for your little tyke!

Step 1 - Start YOUR Day First

The very first step of this whole program is about *you*. As you should now know, you're a rather important part of your little guy's life. He looks to you for guidance, reassurance, protection, and love. When it comes to this long weekend, he'll be following your lead on every step.

If you're happy, he will most likely be fairly happy too. If you're grumpy and you're trying to teach him lovingly, he may get some mixed signals. Mixed signals are never good for a toddler's brain!

So our first step is about you. Wake up (before your toddler, preferably) and get your day started. Take a refreshing shower, get dressed in something comfortable, and brush your teeth so you feel ready for the day ahead.

Drink your first cup of coffee and read the newspaper, get in a quick workout, or whatever your morning routine entails. Do all of this before your little guy wakes up. You want to be as ready as possible by the time he starts his day, so you can kick things off.

As you should know by now, I'm big on preparation. That includes preparing your home for this training, prepping your time for this weekend, preparing yourself (mentally and physically) and now, preparing your little guy.

I advise doing this step every day, not just the first day of this training. As parents, we tend to forget to look after ourselves when we get busy looking after our little ones. But you're important too! This isn't just about time management. This is about looking after yourself, so you can look after your children better.

So, step one: wake up and look after yourself first. Do what you need to or want to, to get ready for the day ahead. You may need to get up an hour earlier so you can get in a workout, or sacrifice a lie-in so you can quickly have a decent breakfast. Don't skip breakfast, either!

If you want to eat breakfast as a family, then wait until your little tyke is up. This could be a great way to start the weekend - a high-fiber breakfast as a family, and then straight into step 2. In fact, step 2 could begin right at the breakfast table!

Step 2 - Get Him Excited About It

You've just spent a month getting your kiddie excited about this every weekend, so it shouldn't take much to get him bouncing around in anticipation today!

When he's awake, greet him enthusiastically and ask him if he remembers what day it is today. It's Big-Boy day!

Once you've had a great, healthy, fiber-packed breakfast, head to his room with his stash of new big-boy underpants. Make a bit of a show of throwing out the diapers. You can get him involved, too! Let him throw one out the door.

Dress him proudly in his big-boy underpants and make a fuss of him and how super he looks. It's important that there's lots of praise at this point, not only word-wise, but using your facial expressions, tone of voice, and gestures.

Remember, kids don't understand language and context yet. They do understand feeling and expression. Think of a clown at a kid's birthday party. Often, there is no talking. But the kids understand exactly what's going on, because of his exaggerated facial expressions, body language, and noises.

That's what you have to do in order to make your toddler feel great. You need to be the clown! It's all fine and well to tell your kiddie that he looks awesome, but unless it's accompanied by lots of excited, wide-eyed expressions, big grins, and a happy tone of voice, he won't understand as well.

Once he's shown off his new undies for a bit and the excitement is starting to settle down, it's time to go get out his new toilet. Remember, he picked it out himself too, so he should have a bit of a bond with it. Of course, toddlers' minds can change in a flash, so if meeting his new toilet again doesn't go down well, don't worry - there are plenty of ways to customize it, as we spoke about in the chapter above.

This is the perfect time to get into the next step.

Step 3 - Explain the Basics

You should be sitting together as a family, with your little guy kitted out in his new undies and looking at his new special toilet. Now is the time to give your child a little bit more information and to give them a role to play in this weekend. If you can swing this to sound like a really fun game, then your kiddie will be a-okay the whole weekend.

Firstly, you need to explain the difference between big-boy underwear and a diaper. Tell your child that he can't pee or poop in big-boy underwear. You may need to get creative in order to get this point across, but you can liken the diaper to a soft, wearable potty if you want an easy comparison.

Then show him how the big-boy underwear needs to *come off* in order to pee in the potty. Make sure he understands this clearly. Don't expect him to have a full understanding of why, or the mechanics behind it, and don't expect him to remember this immediately (or indeed, for a few hours or even a day or so).

The potty is for poop and pee. If you aren't sure that he gets it, a quick and smart trick would be to layer the potty with a diaper.

He already knows what happens in diapers - all he has to do is sit down on the diaper-potty and do his thing.

This worked wonders with my middle child. He realized the diaper was for pooping, so he would go straight to the potty and settle himself on it, on the diaper, and do what he had to do. It was fairly easy to clean most of the time, too - almost just like changing a diaper.

Then, when he was quite used to doing it that way, I simply removed the diaper and laid a thin hand wipe on the bottle of the potty. He took one look and carried on like nothing had changed. Bingo.

Now you'll have to ask him to do something that could be a little hard. He will have to tell you when he starts to feel like he needs to use the potty.

There's a big mistake that parents often make right here. They ask their child to tell them when they need to go, but then they constantly bug their kid by asking "Do you need to go yet?"

Avoid this like the plague. All you need to do is make sure your son knows that if he feels *anything* at *any time* that makes him think he needs to pee or poop, he **must** tell you.

Don't be that nagging parent. The ball is in his court now. Just leave the space open for him to be his own little person and don't hover like you're waiting for him to pee on your shoe!

Carry on with life. You should have some activities planned out to do as a family, so just carry on, keep him fueled with snacks and drinks, and wait.

Step 4 - Be Attentive

Now "just wait" doesn't mean you can leave your little tyke playing with his toys and take a nap while you wait for his fiber-rich foods to kick in and him to tug at your sleeve. Your attentiveness is the **most important part** of this method. Your little guy can't do it without you, so take this role seriously!

It will take some time for your toddler to realize when he needs to pee or poop. It's likely that he'll have an accident or two before he starts to catch on and pay more attention to his body.

Your job is to pay enough attention to be able to catch him in the moment of an accident, pick him up and place him on the nearest potty, so he can finish up.

Yes, you may end up with a trail of pee across the floor. Yes, you may be scrubbing poop out of the carpet. But I assure you, this is an effective way of kick-starting your child's body-brain connection, so they can begin to recognize their own body's signs of needing to go, instead of relying on a diaper or mom or dad to take them to the bathroom.

Things to Remember

If you're not used to spending this much time with your child, day one could be taxing! There will definitely be moments of frustration, times when you roll your eyes and think "Not again," and there may even be an instance where you wonder if you'll ever be toddler-poop-free.

But I can promise, if you work through these moments with patience, love, and determination to get this right, the weekend is going to yield some great results.

Here are some things to remember when the going gets a little tough.

Accidents WILL Happen

As sure as the sun will rise, accidents are going to occur. There is not a doubt in my mind that you *will* have **at least one** accident on the first day. If your kiddie is a super fast learner, one may be all it takes! But most parents are going to have to endure multiple accidents throughout day one that could push at some buttons.

This is where patience, calm, and focus will be most important. It is absolutely crucial that you **don't** respond with anger or frustration when it happens. You want to react with the calmness and serenity of a Zen master, picking up his student to begin again after being beaten by the poop dragon. You get what I mean. Be calm. Expect accidents. Move forward.

Praise Him When He Does It Right

Sometime during the weekend, hopefully on the first day, your little warrior is going to get it right. Your heart will swell with pride and you may have a tearful moment. But instead of turning away, so he doesn't see you cry, give him a huge high-five, do the happy-poop dance (or whatever you and your partner came up with in preparation), and praise him to the roof for getting it right.

Be consistent with your praise too. Have the same reaction every time he gets it right, and when he tries but misses the mark, praise him slightly less enthusiastically, but give him kudos for trying it the right way.

If he's coming close but not quite getting it, remember to reinforce that he needs to tell you when he starts feeling like he needs to go.

Don't just praise him for actually peeing or pooping in the right place, although that definitely needs a good praising. Also praise him when he actually tells you he needs to go. Even if it only yields a drop or it was a false alarm, positive reinforcement is the best way to ensure he does it again.

Be Thoughtful of How You Phrase Things

We've already mentioned that you shouldn't ask your boy outright if he needs to pee or poop. If he puts too much thought into this, he's going to get himself freaked out and the weekend could be a bust.

Remind him every now and then to let you know when he needs to go to the potty. Instead of forcing him to analyze his body and how it feels in a moment by asking *if* he needs to go at the time, you're allowing him the space and freedom to just be, and allow him to become naturally more self-aware.

In this way, he's the one making the big decisions, not you. He's no longer being prompted into it. He's now the big-boy who can tell his mom or dad when he needs to go without being nagged.

Make Sure Your Son is Ready Before Beginning

I know you're most likely reading this the night before you're going to leap into this weekend. But I feel this is such an important point that it's worth rescheduling for (and we've discussed how I feel about procrastinating!).

If your little boy is not ready for this - developmentally and physically - he sure as heck won't be ready for it emotionally.

It is vital that you DO NOT rush into this process just because *you want* your son to be potty-trained.

Rushing into this weekend can have embarrassing, long-lasting, and deeply scarring consequences for a child who simply isn't ready to do this (Dewar, 2010). It can also cause extreme frustration, annoyance, or anger in a parent who isn't getting the results they desire.

Make double, triple sure that your son is showing **two or more** of the signs before starting this process.

Once you're done with day one, it can be tempting to flop into bed and cry...It can be a difficult first day. But, flop into bed and close your eyes immediately. But I advise you to read the next chapter before you go to bed - having it fresh in your mind can only be a good thing!

Chapter 5:

Days Two and Three

Depending on how your day one went, you could be super enthusiastic about day two, or you could be dreading what lies ahead. Don't worry - whichever one you're feeling, I promise it's not abnormal!

Remember to start your day off before your child wakes up. Take a shower, have some coffee, grab a healthy breakfast if you want to eat before your son. It may be a good idea to quickly run through the day's schedule with your partner before your little guy is awake, so you can both be ahead of things from the start.

You're already a third of the way through this potty training mission! It's incredibly important to keep the momentum going today. Yesterday was the foundation for helping your child become self-aware and building up some excitement and confidence.

Today, you're going to be continuing with normal life and waiting for your child to show the signs of needing to go. I find it really helpful to feed him a great breakfast with a drink, and take him straight to the potty when he's finished. He'll remember what it's for, and if he's had a good meal and a drink it's likely that he'll need to go shortly thereafter. This is a good start to the potty training for the day!

It's also a good idea to have a brief discussion with your little boy when he's ready to begin the day and remind him of his successes the day before and encourage him to do the same today.

Positive reinforcement is highly important, so if you can make him good about what he's doing first thing in the morning, it could set a good tone for the whole day (Souders, 2019). As with day one, be excited! It's more important that you stay excited and enthusiastic even if you're feeling a little off. Your mood can and *will* affect your little guy!

I would like to stress that you should have a busy enough schedule that your little guy doesn't find himself bored during the day. Boredom can lead to grumpiness, and we want him to be as happy as possible throughout these three days.

I would advise having a list of activities to fall back on if he loses interest in something or doesn't want to do something that's on your schedule. Some great ideas are:

- Movies or his favorite TV show
- Books - you read to him or get him to read
- Puzzles
- Arts & Crafts
- Drawing or Coloring
- Sports - this could be as simple as throwing a Frisbee around
- Baking - if you can make some high-fiber snacks, even better!

Remember, you need your little dude to be happy and excited about what's happening this weekend. Make sure the activities you've chosen are things that he would enjoy. You know him well, and you know what he likes to do, play with, and spend time on.

Try your hardest not to make this weekend about your own comfort! If he loves building puzzles and you despise it, I'm afraid you're going to have to bite the bullet and push through puzzle-building in order to keep him calm, comfortable, and engaged.

Of course, if there's two of you doing this weekend with your son, you can give each other a break every now and then. Maybe you need to fill up on coffee. Maybe your partner needs a smoke break! Even if you're both really into this and don't feel you need a break, it could be helpful to have mom do something special with her kiddie and dad do something different.

It also breaks up the routine a little for your son, keeping things fresh and interesting and allowing for a bit of bonding time with each parent.

So, remember - start off your own morning before he wakes up, when he's up make sure to offer positive reinforcement and get him excited about the day, and make sure he has a day filled with all the things he enjoys.

Here's what you need to keep in mind through the day:

Steps to Follow Through The Day

It's important that you don't forget what this weekend is about. You may occasionally get distracted doing something fun, but remember everything this weekend has a goal - to get your kiddie to learn how to use the potty.

While the schedule is up to you, and it's a fairly relaxed at-home few days, you need to stick to the small things in order for it to be most effective. Keep it in the back of your mind that you're working towards your child's potty training.

There are a few things you'll need to be quite conscious of as the day goes. It's not difficult to keep them in mind, though. If you do need to check in every couple of hours to make sure you're on the right track, write down a list and leave it somewhere you can check it out every now and then.

In a nutshell:

- Keep him hydrated and fed
- Watch for signs of pee or poop
- Get him to the nearest potty quickly
- Avoid distractions

Keep Him Hydrated & Eating

We've already spoken about high-fiber meals and snacks in a previous chapter. You should have planned meals ahead and stocked up on high-fiber snacks for the whole weekend.

It's very important that you don't worry about your kid eating too much over this weekend. It's just one weekend, and your snacks are going to be fairly healthy as it is. Please avoid things like chips, chocolates, or sugary treats! They're not going to help you reach your goal and are likely to only end in a sugar coma and make your little guy feel lethargic and maybe slightly ill.

It's a good idea to mix and match between high-fiber snacks and watery snacks, making sure that he has enough to drink throughout the day. If your little dude doesn't drink as much as he should, an easy way to get around this is to make it into a game.

- Challenge him to drink his whole glass of juice faster than you.
- Play a game and every time one of you wins, take a sip (and let him win!).
- If you really need to get creative, fill a variety of cups with different colored juice and place them in different spots around the room. Using cards or picking tokens out of a hat, take a sip of whatever color juice matches the color you pick out.

If your kid is one who struggles to eat, you can implement similar strategies to get him to eat his high-fiber snacks.

Remember, you set the example for him. When he gets a high-fiber snack, you get a high-fiber snack. It's essential that you know that you're going to be eating quite a bit and quite often over the weekend!

Breakfast, lunch, and dinner should all be fairly high in fiber and healthy. Aim to have a snack and a glass of juice at least every hour. If you feel that that's not enough, every 30 minutes is all right. You don't need to have a huge snack, either. Share a packet of popcorn for one snack (giving dad the most and little dude the least!). Have a few pieces of dried fruit as the next snack. An hour later, a couple of crackers and one or two slices of cheese would suffice.

Remember, the point of this is to get him to go to the toilet as many times as possible throughout the day, both to poop and pee. His body is still much smaller than yours. While you could go a whole day eating and drinking and not absolutely have to go, he has much less space to store all that waste, so he *will* need to go much more often than you.

Also, he's only now learning how to read the signs of his body - he has no idea how to hold it in when it wants to come out!

Keep an Eye on Him

This doesn't mean you have to stare intently at your child and make sure one of you has eyes on him all day. It just means you need to be attentive and aware of your child's behavior.

Keep your eyes peeled for signs that pee or poop are imminent. Sometimes, there will be no signs. It could surprise both your kiddie and you, and it's important that you don't get frustrated or annoyed when this happens!

Remember, in everything, praise and offer positive reinforcement. Keep the atmosphere of happiness, excitement, fun, and peacefulness.

Here are some things you may notice:
- Squatting
- Restlessness
- Flatulence
- Dancing or jumping on the spot
- Crossing their legs in an unnatural way
- Grabbing or holding their crotch area
- Trying to pull underwear off

Be discerning, though! If the music is on, that dance your toddler is doing could just be him getting in the groove. If the dog is sitting next to you and there's suddenly a bad smell, it could just as likely be the dog as your child!

Don't just rush your child off to the toilet if you see one of these signs. Do, however, gently remind him to let you know when he feels like he needs to go. This isn't nagging, and puts the ball right in his court. It's up to him to make the decision, but if he really does need to go at that moment, your reminder could be welcome and encouraging.

If he doesn't tell you he needs to go, or specifically says he doesn't, don't argue! Remember, this is about your little boy learning how to understand his own body. Don't jump the gun because you feel you know better (it's a very parental thing to do!). If he does have an accident, he won't forget it! He will be more inclined to pay attention and let you know next time if he really does need to go.

Get Him to the Bathroom Quickly (When He Needs to Go)

Once he lets you know that he has to go, don't dawdle. You want to get him to the potty as quickly as you can - remember, he can't hold it in! This is why it's a good idea to start your training with a potty in the room you're in at the time. Once he's learned, you can remove them all except the bathroom one.

If he's not that desperate that he can still walk, lead him to the nearest potty. If he can't quite walk to the bathroom on time, pick him up and take him there. Help him to take off his pants and big-boy underwear, so he can do what he needs to.

If he's already started having an accident, **above all**, stay calm! It may be your instinct to throw your hands in the air, or shout, or display some other kind of impatient, annoyed, or angry behavior. You will need to actively work against letting your instinct get the better of you this weekend!

Stay calm and move him to the potty if you can, so he can finish there. If you can't, that's okay too, but getting him there is definitely first prize. Even when accidents happen, you want him to know that the potty is where he should have been from the start.

If he has an accident, don't be upset with him. Although you shouldn't praise him for almost getting it right, be encouraging and supportive. Do not make him feel bad or like he's let you down. Let him know that next time he should do it all in the potty, not just some of it!

If he managed to get to the potty before he let loose, make a big deal of it! Praise him and if you want to, reward him with a sticker on his chart, a high-five, a toy, or whatever works for him.

Whatever happened, let him watch you clean it up. Take the full potty to the big toilet, empty it out, and let him flush and watch it disappear. This is more effective with poop!

Make Sure There Are No Distractions

As you can tell, there's likely to be a lot of waiting, watching, and running to the potty in these three days. This is why it's incredibly important to avoid distractions! This is actually more for the parents than for the child. He's going to need to pee or poop no matter what he's doing. This is about *you* being attentive enough to help your child reach this milestone.

Of course, you can't make life stand still for the whole weekend. But things like visits, phone calls, social media, cleaning the house, or spending time on your own hobbies isn't going to work for these three days (sorry!).

You really need to make every moment of this weekend about your son and getting him over this hurdle. You've already let friends and family know that you're doing this and won't be available for chatting or hanging out, so stick to that.

Please know that I'm not encouraging you to ignore everybody else and avoid outside life entirely! I'm well aware that emergencies happen, so you can only do so much to keep distractions at bay.

If you do need to take a call, go for it but keep it brief. Make sure your partner is there to keep an eye on your little guy while you're talking. If you have to make coffee, reply to a message, take a short walk to stretch your legs, or check your email quickly, then do so!

Just don't leave your son coloring while you get sucked into your Facebook feed. Don't take a phone call and chat for half an hour with your best friend, while your son draws a picture.

Remember, he's most likely going to need a nap sometime during the day too, so you will have a bit of time to catch up on things you may need or want to do.

Things to Keep in Mind

While this day is mostly about building a habit in your child very quickly, there are other aspects of potty training that you should pay attention to and reinforce as the day goes. Remember, using the potty is a behavioral thing. It's great to teach your kid how to listen to his body and go in the right place, but there are other behavioral things that are important in the big picture.

Hygiene is of utmost importance. You want your child to stay as healthy as possible! While it may seem like potty training is the least hygienic thing in the world (poop on the carpet, pee on the wall…) it's essential that you begin to teach your child some of the components of staying hygienic when they're still learning how to use the potty.

These habits will be instilled together. Have you ever been in a public restroom and seen someone exit a stall and head straight out without so much as glancing at the faucet and soap? You don't want that to be your kid one day.

Hygiene habits are as important as the actual potty habit, and now is the best time to teach them. Instill all those habits together, so your son can associate them with each other from a young age.

Hand Washing

Please don't neglect this action! It's such an important part of staying healthy and hygienic and it's honestly not very hard to do.

The first step is to make sure that your child **sees you** washing your hands after you've been to the toilet. Kids follow by example. If you don't wash your hands, how can you tell your kid to? They're smarter and more intuitive than we realize, and they may not regard it as important if they see you brushing it off.

Make a show of putting soap on your hands and washing it off, rubbing your hands together well. You could even get your child his own bottle of hand wash and teach him how the pump action works. Then he has his own toilet *and* his own soap!

Bear in mind that you will probably have to make use of a small step for your son to reach the basin. Make certain that it's a sturdy step and stands on a level bit of the floor. Although you will be with your son every time he washes his hands on these three days, the goal is to have him coming to the potty by himself, and that means washing his hands by himself too.

You want everything in the bathroom to be as safe as possible. Place a rubber mat under the step so there's far less chance of it slipping out from under him while he's climbing it.

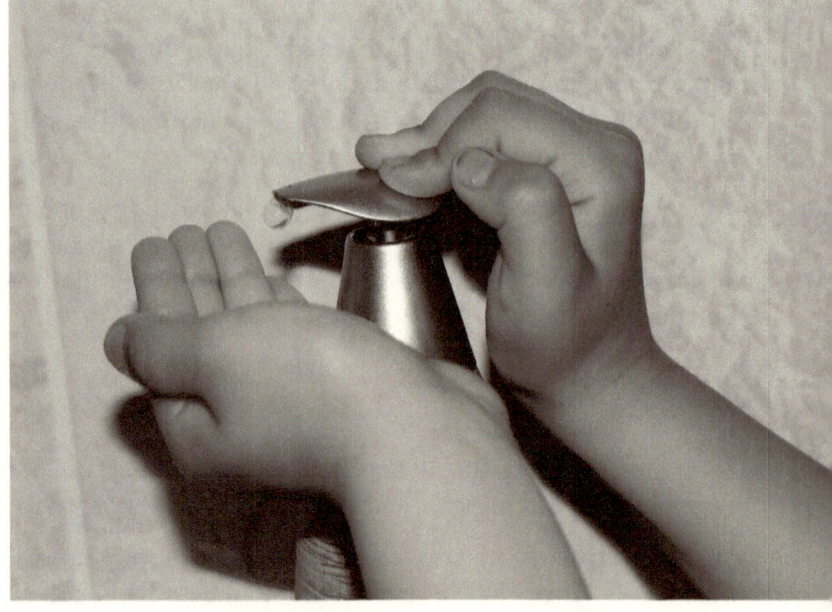

Image by ali güler from Pixabay

Wiping

Remember, your little tyke has had the fortune of you cleaning him up after messy poops. Until now, he's never had to clean himself up, so this may need a bit of work to get it right.

Don't be alarmed if the first time he poops on the potty, he gets up and tries to wander off without wiping when he's done. He doesn't know that he needs to clean himself up!

If he's been watching mom, he'll know that wiping happens, even if he couldn't tell you why or what exactly you're doing. Even dad wipes sometimes, so it's not a completely unusual thing to him.

You'll need to explain to him that this is important to stay clean. You'll need to demonstrate how to do this properly for your little guy. You can do that by standing behind him, placing the toilet paper in his hand, and guiding his hand to wipe. Kids learn quite well by being shown, so this should do the trick. You may need to show him more than once, and remember you'll also need to explain to him that he only needs to do this when he makes a poop!

Now, just as proper form is important to prevent injury in sport, proper wiping form is essential too. It may sound odd, but if done wrong, your little one could be more at risk of bacterial infections.

"Front to back" is what we're aiming for. Why? Well, it wipes all the nasty stuff towards the back, *away* from all the other important bits in the area. Although your child is going to be bathed, it's best to make sure there's as little chance as possible of bacteria making a home.

Monitor him carefully as he learns to wipe on his own. If he starts doing it the wrong way, gently guide him back to the "front to back" movement and give him the necessary praise when he gets it right.

Imitation

We've also spoken quite a bit about how little children learn by watching and mimicking (Meltzoff, 1999). This is true for everything from playing, walking, and interacting with others to… Yes, how to go potty.

One of the preparation steps is to invite your child's curiosity and allow them to watch while you or your partner go to the toilet. You may have had some questions, or you may have had nothing, but either way, they take it in.

Don't let this stop now. When dad has to go to the bathroom, let your little guy go with. If he has a big brother, do the same (after asking big brother's permission, of course). Now that he's actually doing it for himself, he may look at it with a different kind of interest to before.

This is the perfect time to show him how to aim! If you search a little, you can get little "waterproof" stickers to stick inside the toilet bowl that he can aim at when he's busy. This could be fun and help prevent him spraying all over the place if he gets distracted with stuff around him.

It's important that your little guy understands that he shouldn't sit and pee. It should be clear to him from the start that standing if for pee, sitting is for poop. Again, this may be easiest to demonstrate physically, and he may wonder why mom apparently never pees. But if you get him in the habit of sitting down at this stage, it's difficult to retrain him later.

Remember, imitation extends to wand washing, drying, flushing, and cleaning. He needs to see these things happen in order to know what to do. If he's able to, encourage him to help clean his own potty when he's done.

Potty training doesn't only involve the "where to pee and poop" training! It's about hygiene, and flushing, hand washing, and keeping the environment clean are all important parts of it.

Positive Reinforcement

Positive reinforcement must be the thing you use the most over this weekend. You may be quite tired of it by the time the weekend is over! While it's important not to completely overdo it, you'll want to praise your child when:

- He lets you know he needs to go
- He gets to the potty in time
- He can pull his pants down by himself
- He positions himself correctly on the potty
- He pees or poops in the potty (even if he messes a little)
- He flushes when he's done
- He washes his hands and dries them

It's important **not** to praise your child when he has an accident. Of course, you're not going to punish him or shame him. In these cases, use neutral language - neither praising nor shaming.

While a successful potty experience may get "Yay! You did it all by yourself! You're so smart!" accompanied by the potty dance, an accident may get something like "You peed on the floor. Help me clean it up, and we can try again next time."

Never punish your child for having an accident. Punishing includes:

- Yelling at your child
- Smacking him
- Shaming him or making him feel bad about himself
- Embarrassing him in front of other people
- Calling him stupid or telling him he will never learn

You may be gasping in shock and horror at the thought of some parents doing these things to their children, but it does happen. Even the most well-meaning of parents can lose their temper sometimes and raise their voice.

You could have woken up with a slight headache, your breakfast didn't taste so good, and your spouse is annoyingly cheerful after they kept you up all night with their snoring. You're already in a worse mood, and after seeing poop on the carpet for the fourth time today you may just lose control a little and lash out. Even something as small as sighing loudly and rolling your eyes *will* be noticed by your child!

You need to stick to positive reinforcement in all ways, especially those that matter most to a child - verbal, body language, and facial expressions. If you're telling him it's okay but your tone of voice and angry eyes are saying it really isn't, he's not only going to feel confused, but ashamed too.

If you feel you're getting close to blowing up or saying something you shouldn't, take a fiver. Ask your partner to look after him for a few minutes and take a walk, call a friend to vent, have some coffee, or take a quick drive around the block to clear your head and cool down.

It's imperative that you calm down and come back with the right attitude. Your child's success over this weekend depends hugely on you! When he gets praise, attention, and affection, he does things well because he wants to please. But if he gets eye rolls, sighs, yells, or even just angry facial expressions, he'll feel confused, anxious, and most likely not get things right because he's afraid of disappointing you.

Don't think that your son being afraid of disappointing you is going to get him to do it better than if he's pleasing you! Some parents feel that scaring children into doing things right is the way to go. It *could* be effective, I won't deny that. But wouldn't you rather your child gets through this experience being surrounded by love and patience rather than annoyance and fear?

Remember, this is just one of the many milestones your child will go through. If you start with anger and fear, it's hard to win your child's trust back later if you decide to change. If you start with love, caring, and encouragement, it will set him up for better success without breaking bonds.

Getting Out of the House

If you feel like day two is going well, you can attempt to include an outside excursion in your schedule. This doesn't have to be far - it could even be just in the yard for the time being. The idea is to get your child used to these feelings in different places, at different times, and even perhaps when surrounded by other people.

As a comparison, it's great to learn to speak a foreign language. But if you only ever spoke it to your parents, you'd only be getting half the experience, half the benefit. If you went out and spoke to other people, you'd learn so much quicker and gain confidence, too.

No learning is most effective in a closed, controlled environment. If you want to really solidify what you've learned, getting out into an uncontrolled environment is best. A variety of environments is even better.

If you don't feel your child is quite ready for outdoor excursions, that's okay. You know them best, and you've been spending this weekend with them so you understand the progress they're making.

If you want a halfway point, the yard is a good start. It's far enough away from the potty that it's like a mini outdoor excursion.

Prepare

Don't decide on the spur of the moment that you want to leave the house, though. This warrants a bit of preparation.

Backyard Excursions

If you're starting out in the backyard, you don't even need to take a potty with you. It's still a safe space for your little guy, so if he has an accident, it won't be an issue. Of course, if you have a communal backyard, then I would suggest applying some caution!

If you're in your own backyard, spend some time outside doing any kind of activity he likes. Kick a ball, throw a ball, play with the dog, take a swim. Make sure he's engaged enough to be outside for 20 to 30 minutes.

Remember to either take a snack and drink outside with you or have him eat and drink just before you head outside. Ideally, you want your toddler to realize that he needs to go while he's outside and away from the potty entirely.

In order to make this as successful as possible:

- Plan the activity, and have a backup in case he gets bored.
- Feed him a snack and drink before heading outside or shortly after.
- Get him engaged in outdoor activity for 20 to 30 minutes.
- Be prepared for an accident.

If you don't have the potty with you and you're further away from it than usual, the potential for accidents is higher. That's okay! If your son poops or pees outside it's not as big a deal as if he does it inside. Don't disregard it, though. Speak to him the same way you would if it was indoors. If he lets you know he needs to go, praise him and take him to the potty as quickly as possible.

If 20 to 30 minutes have passed and nothing has happened, it's up to you what to do. You could hang around outside a bit more and wait, but if he's getting antsy and a little bored then this may not be possible.

You could head inside and carry on from there. If this happens, I'd chalk it up to a mild success! No accidents are always a win.

Off The Property

If you're feeling brave and like your little guy can handle it, you can take short trips out and about off the property. I'd advise not deciding to go grocery shopping, visit a friend, or take a long car trip. These outings should also be 20 to 30 minutes long, including any time spent in the car.

You can take the potty with you, but it's probably best not to walk around with it in your hand. Leave it in the car while you're out, and if he does tell you he needs to go, fetch it.

Also, if he does need to go, and he gets to the potty, make sure he's hidden from public view. We don't want him being embarrassed in public and forever having a negative association with going to the toilet!

The same is true for if he has an accident. Move him out of the public eye and clean him up. It may be worth taking a small folding screen with you if you have one or can get one.

Regardless of where you go or what you do:

- Be prepared for accidents.
- Take extra clothes with you.
- If necessary, take cleaning up stuff along.
- Keep your positive reinforcement going.
- Don't be out for longer than 30 minutes, even if he hasn't had an accident or indicated that he needs to go.
- Make sure your child isn't in a position where he could be embarrassed.
- When you get home, praise him for doing well during the outing.

Be Quick

If you're worried about being out of the house for too long, try just 10 to 15 minutes in the yard at first. If it goes well, you can up it to 20 to 30 minutes.

Give it some proper time, though. Don't pop outside for 5 minutes and then rush him back inside. Allow *at least* 10 minutes outside.

If you're going to be out and about, choose where and what you're doing carefully. Having social visits, shopping trips, or any other outings in crowded areas could be a problem. An outdoor area that is away from the home, quiet, and away from crowds is perfect.

While it may sound contradictory to tell you to be quick and then say not to rush it, the timing of this step is important! You want to be outside just long enough for your child's bodily process to kick in, but not so long that they actually have an accident.

Don't expect to get it spot on the first time. Although you don't have a lot of time to be out and about, either in one go or for multiple outdoor visits in one weekend, it's a good idea to do at least three or four outdoor excursions over the weekend; two on Saturday, two on Sunday.

Be Calm

It's essential that parents don't get freaked out by this step! It can be exhaustively anticipatory, taking your child out and basically waiting for an accident to happen. Parents may be so worried about their child pooping in public that they rush through this step, or even avoid it entirely.

Your confidence is important in order to get this right. Act as though you're doing something completely normal, and your child will be at ease if you're just your normal self.

Keep calm and carry on. If your kid tugs on your sleeve and says they need to go, stay calm, praise them, and get to the potty. If an accident happens, stay calm, keep your language neutral, and clean them up. Keep your actions relaxed and like any other day.

If you aren't sure what to do to get out of the house and don't want to just wander around the store, here are some ideas:

- Take the dog for a walk.
- Visit the park and kick a ball around.
- Do some garden work (this is great for the first outing - it's "out of the house" but not too far away).
- Go to the store if you need to.
- Have a very short visit with a friend (yours or your boy's!).

Photo by Gustavo Fring from Pexels

Chapter 6:

Going Forward

Once you've made it past the 3-day challenge, it can be tempting to put it behind you and forget it ever happened. I know it's a taxing experience! As much as your child may have loved a weekend dedicated entirely to his enjoyment and being waited on hand and foot with snacks and drinks, it's not a fun, relaxed few days for parents.

But you can't put this behind you and hope your kiddie carries on acting like a big-boy. You need to be actively involved in this process going forward - it didn't just end after day 3!

Just because your little guy can use the toilet at home, it doesn't mean he's fully trained. Daycare may be hard for him, and it's very likely there will still be multiple accidents in the weeks and months to come.

Going forward after the 3 days can be challenging. The weekend comes with many feelings - excitement, frustration, anticipation, happiness, defeat. Your little dude should have made some real progress! You should be going forward happy and proud of your little man.

This is the mindset you need to cling to in the coming weeks. Remember all the progress he's made and how well he's done. If he continues with just as much success, that's fantastic! If he has a few accidents, there's nothing to worry about. It's normal, and to be expected.

In some cases, the child can regress to the point of not being able to go without a diaper again. This is not common, so don't freak yourself out about it happening.

If it does happen, though, it doesn't mean you failed, or your child is broken. Not at all! It just means some research is warranted to figure out exactly what the problem is and how to fix it. Regression can be triggered by certain factors, and it can almost always be fixed quickly.

Going forward, you need to stay vigilant and involved in the process.

Observe

Although you'll be going back to work and your child will be going to daycare again, you'll still have opportunities to observe his behavior. Weekends would be the perfect time to observe, practice, and reinforce what he's learned.

Most importantly, continue to offer positive reinforcement over time. Just because you're not spending the whole weekend waiting for your son to poke you and tell you he needs to go, it doesn't mean he doesn't value your encouragement and praise! If you suddenly act like this toilet training thing was nothing important, the poor kid is going to be confused and somewhat upset.

Keep encouraging! Observe how he responds to your encouragement. If he responds well, keep doing what you're doing. If something changes in his response or his behavior, some detective work may be necessary to figure out what the problem is.

If you've been open with your son until this point, he should be comfortable with you being in the bathroom while he's busy. You should also be comfortable with him being in there while you're busy.

Allow him to keep observing if he needs to, and sneak observe him while he's on the potty too. Make sure he's doing things as he should be and doesn't need help. Don't walk in behind him and stand and stare while he's busy, though. Act natural and wash your hands or look in the bathroom cupboard for something.

Observation is important, not only to keep an eye on if he's doing it right but to make sure he's still happy and comfortable.

If you notice that he's missing the potty when he pees, invest in "toilet target" decals to help him to aim. This gamifies the process a little and makes it more fun to learn, as well as keeping his attention where it needs to be - in the toilet, and not on the wall, floors, or carpets.

Let It Evolve

It can be tempting to assume that your kiddie is an expert potty-er now, and expect him to do it right every time from then on.

But remember, these are just the basics. Your toddler may be more than happy to do their thing in the potty, but may have trouble going in the big toilet. You may never realize this if they're constantly using the potty and not attempting the big toilet at home!

For this reason, it's a good idea to keep "training" even after the 3 days. Once they've got the potty down, start focusing more on the big toilet with the toddler toilet seat attachment.

Allow your child's toilet evolution to proceed naturally. If they're nervous about the big toilet, don't push them. Employ the same techniques used throughout the 3 days - let them figure it out on their own, with you there to provide support and encouragement.

One of the best ways to get this started, though, is using public toilets. Even if your little one is slowly getting into it at home, they may not be happy with using a public toilet. If you're like most moms and have a Mary Poppins bag to carry all your toddler's stuff, it's easy to get a portable toilet seat attachment to take with you when out in public.

You can try the "feed, water, and wait" method before you head to the shop. Give your child a high-fiber snack and some juice before you go, take your toilet seat with, and wait for them to let you know that they have to go.

It's important that you only try this once you're little one is quite familiar with the potty, though! If they're still quite new, they may prefer to try and hold it in, which could lead to an accident.

Once they've been able to go on the toilet seat in a public toilet (because the only other choice was an accident), they may be more inclined to use it at home.

Another reason this could be happening is that they're afraid of the height of the toilet. You may need to find other ways of tackling this fear before they'll be happy to use the big toilet by themselves, especially if your child is small for his age.

Also, most toddlers won't be able to hold it in through the night for at least a few months after learning to use the potty. You could let him wear a nappy at night, and help him dress in his big-boy undies for the day ahead.

Keep in mind that every child's development will be different. You'll need to be attentive and observe your child as time passes to see where his weaknesses lie. You can adapt your post-3-day training to pinpoint exactly what he's struggling with, but remember that he doesn't need to be "fixed." You're just guiding him along his path until he can figure these things out for himself.

Expect Accidents

Accidents are going to happen, and there's nothing you can do to prevent them. They don't mean that something is wrong with your child. They don't mean that you've failed as a parent! They also don't mean that the 3-day method failed.

In the weeks following the 3-day mission weekend, your child's body and brain will be busy readjusting themselves to deal with what they've learned. Sometimes there will be crossed signals.

Maybe your child is playing and feels an inkling, but doesn't want to stop. Before he knows it, he can't hold it in anymore, and he's not close to the potty. Or maybe he's out in public and is shy to tell you that he needs to go.

Maybe he's simply not paying attention and lets his body release, forgetting that he's not wearing a diaper.

Whatever the reason, I can assure you that every accident that happens is one closer to being the last one.

The 3-day process is not something that solidifies this habit. It builds a fantastic foundation for your child to start getting used to it and understanding how to listen to his own body.

But the learning doesn't stop when the weekend ends. In fact, it's only beginning - in the real world. Training in a controlled place with few potential outcomes is one thing, but being out and about in strange places where the potty isn't just round the corner and there are other people around is a little harder.

It's still imperative that you offer positive reinforcement and do not punish your child if he has an accident. Be patient, be kind, and be calm. It's perhaps even more important to be patient with your child now than it was over the 3 days. If you react badly to an accident now, he may start to feel pressure and anxiety that he's not doing well enough, which could actually lead to a regression.

Keep it loving!

What to Do

- **Be Prepared**

To deal with accidents, preparation is key. Always expect that there *may* be an accident, but have faith that it won't happen.

Keep a change of clothes, cleaning supplies, and plastic bags with you for dirty clothes. Wet wipes are invaluable, as is hand sanitizer spray.

- **Stay Calm**

Don't cause a scene or draw attention to yourself or your child. He's likely to be feeling embarrassed and upset already, and drawing more attention to him will only make things worse.

Quietly remove him from the public space, covering him with your own jacket if possible and necessary. Clean him up, keeping him calm too!

- **Don't Punish Your Child**

Punishing can be damaging. You'll know by now that I'm a huge advocate of positive reinforcement and getting things done with love, kindness and patience!

In all my own potty training experiences and those of friends and family that I've been fortunate enough to help with, it's struck me that kindness has been far more effective than anger.

It can be tempting to yell, smack, or shake your child if an accident happens, purely because it's extremely frustrating after all your work.

But trust the process and trust your child! Allow him the space to work it out, knowing that he has loving and supportive parents by his side.

Regression

On occasion, a child who has been potty-trained effectively will revert back to needing to wear a diaper. This isn't very common, and it's a completely different thing to having an accident.

If your child has a few accidents, it doesn't mean they need to go back in a diaper. If your child suddenly develops a fear of the toilet or potty, and has an accident every single they go, this is more concerning and could be a real regression.

Regressions don't just happen randomly. There's usually a triggering factor that causes the child to revert, and it's figuring that out that can be difficult.

If you are dealing with a regression, I know it can be crushing. You've put your "blood, sweat, and tears" into this process, and it seems like it's all been for nothing. Rest assured, your hard work hasn't gone to waste!

Remember, the 3-day method is a foundation that needs to be built upon later. That foundation has been ingrained in your child, and although a regression may suppress it for a while, those foundations remain and can be accessed later once the regression has been dealt with.

I can tell you that as hard as it is for you, it's ten times harder for your child. It's tempting to assume that he's just being lazy and doesn't want to go to the potty when he needs to, so he's just being stubborn. While it's possible, it would be an extremely unusual case!

He may be feeling anxious and ashamed. He knows how important this is to his parents - after all, you spent a whole weekend with him teaching him! He may be young, but toddlers are smarter than we know.

So, what do we do when a child regresses?

What to Do

- **Be Patient**

Patience is incredibly important in this situation. You'll need to suppress the urge to show annoyance, anger, or frustration.

I'd like to highlight that fact that you **are allowed** to feel annoyed, frustrated, and hopeless! These feelings are completely normal and there's nothing wrong with you having them. You're only human!

The most important thing is that no matter how you feel, you display nothing but calm, love, and patience.

It's not easy. But it's crucial for your child.

- **Don't Punish Your Child**

As always, no punishment. Because you've seen such great progress before, it can be tempting to assume that he's just being a stubborn little guy and playing games with you.

But in general, children don't go to such lengths to be lazy! Imagine walking around with a wet, sludgy, smelly mass in your underwear. It can't be comfortable at all. Why would your child do that just because they're being lazy?

There's a legitimate reason for your child to be behaving this one. Be patient and don't make the situation worse by adding punishment on top of the shame your little guy may already be feeling.

- **Stick to Positive Reinforcement**

You may be wondering how to positively reinforce a regression. It's not a positive step, so how do you keep up positive reinforcement?

It's a good question, and not always easy to answer. You can't praise your child for regressing. But you certainly shouldn't treat them in a negative way.

Neutrality is the best way to go. No praise, no punishment, but quiet support and encouragement that you know they can do this.

Don't try and encourage your child by telling them you know they can do it because they did it before. This could be helpful later on when re-teaching them, but right now it could make them feel worse about it as they should be expected to get it right.

- **Ask Your Child Why It Happened**

If your child regresses, don't ignore it. Talk it through if your little one can have a conversation. Try to determine what changed in your child's life to cause this regression.

The heart of regression is anxiety. Something as simple as being embarrassed at daycare about their potty habits could cause your child enough anxiety to regress.

It's important to understand that this is a trauma. Not necessarily a physical one, but something has caused your little guy to become so anxious that he can't bring himself to do what he used to be able to.

If he can't tell you, some detective work may be necessary. Ask the daycare staff, his nanny, or his friends' parents if anything unusual has happened.

Sometimes you won't get a definitive answer. It's frustrating, but there's not much you can do. Simply continue to be supportive and patient and wait for when it's safe and comfortable to re-train.

- **Start Training Again**

You'll need to start training from the beginning again. Your child may know what's going on this time, but you'll just be providing them an opportunity to get their anxiety under control and allow their body to get back into the habit.

Take it slow and be extra patient and loving.

- **If Necessary, See Your Child's Doctor**

If you're extremely worried about the regression or can't find a real reason for it, a trip to the pediatrician may be a good idea. In some cases, there could be a medical reason behind the regression, and if you've ruled out any other reasons a check-up could reveal some insight.

Common Problems (And Solutions)

Like any learning curve, there are some common problems that parents may run into during the process. They're usually harmless and can be fixed with a little work.

But they can cause extreme frustration and make us feel like the method isn't working, or we're doing something wrong.

In most cases, you're not doing anything wrong! If you've been following the tips and tricks in this book, you're most likely doing things to the "T" and getting them right.

It also doesn't mean that your kid is unteachable or a problem child. It just means that you'll need to work a little harder to overcome these and make your child feel comfortable.

Here are some common problems that you may run into when teaching your child to use the toilet.

Your Son Doesn't Recognize When He Needs to Pee

Some kids find it really easy to recognize when they need to poop, but can't quite feel when they need to pee. Don't worry! This is quite normal.

Consider that pooping can sometimes come with pain, discomfort, and gassiness. These are sure signs that a poop is imminent, and your child may be able to pick these signs up much quicker than the feeling of a full bladder.

In fact, your child could learn bowel control and recognition months before they get bladder control right.

Don't worry if this seems to be an issue. Keep teaching like you normally would, and this should sort itself out. Patience will be necessary, though!

Don't assume that your child isn't learning properly or doing something wrong or being stubborn. This is all about the body and their developing body-brain-body connections.

The body sends a signal from the organ to the brain telling it that something is happening. The brain interprets the signal, decides how to react appropriately, and sends a signal back to the body, resulting in pressure, pain, or discomfort.

As adults, our brains and bodies are so used to this that it happens completely naturally and in a split second. Kids, though, haven't quite got it down to a fine art yet. It's quite easy for one of those steps along the way to go a little wonky.

Because bowel movements are so much more noticeable than bladder movements, it's not unrealistic to assume that pooping is much easier to detect. The urge to pee is much more subtle, and could be easily missed.

He Resists Going to the Bathroom

It's important to realize the difference between resistance being potty-trained and being distracted. Most information you'll find says that if your child resists going to the bathroom, he's not ready to be potty-trained.

In a way, this is true. If he's displaying signs that he is ready, like showing interest in the toilet, wanting to remove his diapers, and being able to have a clean diaper for 2 hours or more, it's likely that he's ready. But that's not absolute.

But what we're talking about here is when your son is potty-trained but frequently has accidents because he's distracted and leaves it too late to get to the toilet in time!

This can be quite common, especially for kids who are very active. They're getting a good handle on listening to their body, but when they're engaged in an activity that's interesting to them, they could put it out of their mind and realize too late that they can't get to a toilet.

This will get better as they develop. As their body develops, they'll be able to hold it in for longer. But it's more likely that they'll eventually start feeling these things even when they're busy. After many accidents, they will begin to realize that it's a problem and their body will correct it on its own.

He's Afraid of the Toilet

This is usually actually a fear of being sucked into the toilet when it flushes. The sound and the churning water can be terrifying to a little person. Think about it - for us adults, that's the toilet flushing. For a 2-foot tall toddler, that's a tsunami that's coming to get them. Remember, their imaginations are also so much more active than ours!

You can help reduce this fear by allowing him to flush the toilet while you're sitting on it. He'll be able to see that you don't get sucked away, and this will put his mind at ease.

You could also allow him to flush away pieces of toilet paper, so he gets used to how it works and the sound of it flushing. Be warned, though - this could lead to a fun new hobby for your child. You may find that car keys, cellphones, goldfish, snacks, socks, and a variety of other things end up being flushed away!

He Tries to Play With His Pee or Poop

Kiddies are curious! They may actually never have seen their poop up close before. They're used to pooping and having you remove it and throw it away without them even seeing it.

When they first spot it in their potty, they may be quite fascinated by this stuff. It's not disgusting, creepy, or cause for concern. It's just a child being a child.

It is important to catch this early on, though, and explain that it's not something to be played with.

You should be staying with your child during potty training until the poop is flushed away and the potty is clean. Any attempt to play with their poop should be quite easily noticed, so you can get a handle on it early.

It may not be easy to dissuade your kiddie from playing with it. You can't explain it logically to a toddler. In some cases, telling your toddler *not* to play with it is only going to make him want to play with it more!

If this is an issue, I suggest making a big deal of how you dispose of the poop so your kiddie can see that you're actively trying **not** to touch it.

Remember to exaggerate your facial expressions and body language. Pick up the potty and pretend to look at the poop, then quickly look away and make a face. Pretend to sniff it and make a worse face!

Empty the poop into the toilet, taking care not to touch it. If you need to do some work to remove it, emphasize every movement and **make sure he sees you** trying not to touch it.

If you see his hand snake towards it, smack it lightly and make a face. Don't do this in a nasty way! It's meant to be a light gesture to show that you're protecting him from something nasty.

Keep at it, and he should soon get bored with trying to play with it. Also, at some point, the smell should put him off!

He'll Only Go to the Toilet With One Particular Person

If you've spent time during preparation taking your son to the toilet with you when you go and your partner has done the same, this shouldn't be a problem at home.

The issue can come in when your child goes back to daycare, or spends time at a friend's house, and mom and dad aren't there to take him to the toilet.

If you've found out that this is the case, you'll need to start withdrawing yourself slowly from the potty process. Start leading your child to the bathroom, but waiting outside while they go. That way, they'll be comforted by your presence but also build up confidence that they can do this by themselves.

Tell them that anybody can take them to the bathroom door. If they don't want them to come inside, they can tell them to wait outside the door. Work on this with another family member or close friend that your son knows but doesn't trust quite that well.

It's also worth explaining to your child that if they don't know the person at all, they should never go to the bathroom with them or ask them to take them to the bathroom. Stranger danger is always relevant!

Photo by Pixabay

Conclusion

Potty training doesn't have to be complicated or cause nightmares! It's perfectly possible to do it effectively, with as little stress as possible, and in a loving, fun way - and in just a weekend!

Don't just take my word for it, either. Here are some reviews from real live parents who've had success with this method (*3 Day Potty Training Review » Potty Training a Stubborn Child*, n.d.):

- "I have tried 4 different times to potty-train my stubborn 2-year-old. Your 3-day thing totally worked!" - Rosie

- "I was searching the internet for training methods and ran across your book. We went to the store in her padded panties and purchased everything that we needed. She had a LOT of accidents that day. I figured it was a giant failure but stuck with it. The next day we had two accidents in the morning and NONE the rest of the day. The next morning she woke up dry and has stayed that way ever since. A little less than a day and half, and she's all done. Thanks a million!" - Andrea

- "A few months ago I read your website about potty training and bought your E-Book and prepared myself for the potty training of my 2 1/2 year old stubborn son. It was the Easter weekend that I planned all this for and the weather was lovely. My partner was off from work too and working in the garden. Day three was a great success, and he was wearing stickers on all his clothes for being such a good boy. No accidents and he received his presents with pride! Day four we went to two separate supermarkets, and he went to the toilet in one and stayed in the trolley during the other shop and went to the toilet as soon as we got home. This was my biggest challenge, and we managed it brilliantly and I could shout this from the rooftops. I AM SO HAPPY." - Yvonne

It's a fact - the 3-day method works! (for stubborn children as well as easygoing ones). By setting aside 3 days of your time and focusing entirely on your child, you're teaching him exactly how to listen to his own body. You've just helped him take a step closer to becoming a fully independent little human!

Using this method allows your child to come to these realizations without being pushed or forced. It's all about helping your child understand what's happening and how to counter it. Once he knows that he can't just go to the toilet in his pants, it's as simple as getting that switch to flip in his brain.

There's no forcing. There's no humiliation. There's just a weekend filled with fun with mom and dad, great snacks, plenty of play, and a new skill.

Are you ready to put dirty diapers behind you forever? Who isn't! You have these amazing tools right at your fingertips (literally), so go out there and put them to good use.

When your child surprises you with their toilet prowess, I'd love to hear about it! Please leave a review on Amazon if this book has helped the process, and let me know just how well your little guy is doing.

Best of luck and remember - do it all with love!

References

3 Day Potty Training Review » potty training a stubborn child. (n.d.). 3 Day Potty Training. Retrieved August 24, 2020, from http://www.3daypottytraining.com/w/t/potty-training-a-stuborn-child/

Bureau of Labor. (2020). EMPLOYMENT CHARACTERISTICS OF FAMILIES -2019. https://www.bls.gov/news.release/pdf/famee.pdf

Choby, B. A., & George, S. (2008). Toilet Training. American Family Physician, 78(9), 1059–1064. https://www.aafp.org/afp/2008/1101/p1059.html#:~:text=Spock

Dewar, G. (2010). The science of toilet training: What research tells us about timing. www.Parentingscience.com. https://www.parentingscience.com/science-of-toilet-training.html

Meltzoff, A. N. (1999). Born to Learn: What Infants Learn from Watching Us. http://ilabs.washington.edu/meltzoff/pdf/99Meltzoff_BornToLearn.pdf

National Center for Biotechnology Information. (2019). Potty training: Overview. In www.ncbi.nlm.nih.gov. Institute for Quality and Efficiency in Health Care (IQWiG). https://www.ncbi.nlm.nih.gov/books/NBK279296/#:~:text=Research%20suggests%20that%20it%20could

Souders, B. (2019, July 4). Parenting Children with Positive Reinforcement (Examples + Charts). PositivePsychology.com.

https://positivepsychology.com/parenting-positive-reinforcement/

www.ingramcontent.com/pod-product-compliance
Lightning Source LLC
Chambersburg PA
CBHW021428070526
44577CB00001B/110